13 Ways to Save

The Power of Coupons

*"Have plenty to eat, until you are full, and
you will praise the name of the Lord your God,
who has worked wonders for you."*
Joel 2:26

Sarah Roe

918 Coupon Queen

insight
PUBLISHING GROUP

The Power of Coupons: 13 Ways to Save
© 2010 by Sarah Roe

Published by
Insight Publishing Group
8801 South Yale, Suite 410
Tulsa, Oklahoma 74137
918-493-1718

Unless otherwise noted, all Scripture quotations are taken from the *Holy Bible, New International Version.* Copyright © 1973, 1978, 1984 by International Bible Society. Used by permission of Zondervan Publishing House. All rights reserved.

Scripture quotations marked NKJV are taken from the *New King James Version of the Bible,* Copyright © 1982 by Thomas Nelson, Inc.

Scripture quotations marked AMP are taken from the *Amplified Bible,* Copyright © 1954, 1958, 1962, 1964, 1965, 1987 by the Lockman Foundation. Used by permission. All rights reserved.

Scripture quotations marked KJV are taken from the *King James Version* of the Bible.

ISBN 978-1-932503-86-9

Library of Congress catalog card number: 2009936061

Printed in the United States of America.

Dedication

To my husband, Eric, and my two little boys, Elisha and Ethan. I love you. You are my princes.

Table of Contents

Acknowledgements

I can still remember standing in our living room in our little old house, asking my husband how he would feel if I started teaching a few coupon classes. He told me he would support anything I did as long as I felt God was leading me to do it—and as long as I stuck with it long enough to let God bless it. It has been a whirlwind ever since. I want to say thank you to my husband, Eric, for encouraging and believing in me and to my two little boys, Elisha and Ethan, for being my biggest fans!

I also want to thank our families for helping us through this journey, and my dad, the original Coupon King. I can still remember being a teenager and my dad handing me a coupon while I headed out the door. You are the best deal a girl could find!

Thanks to my Grandma Bonnie for being my biggest coupon supplier and clipping service—God will literally bless the "work of your hands"! And also to Trudy for your faithful coupon drop-offs that made it possible for me to share coupons with families all across our city. Thanks to all the 918 Coupon Princesses for your hours of hard work posting matchups and deals and helping me share these awesome techniques with thousands.

Thank you to Melanie Henry, Deedra Determan, and David Griffin for taking a chance on a mom with coupons. Your amazing ideas and creativity opened the door for thousands of people to hear the teachings that have saved them hundreds of dollars each month! I can still hear Melanie and Deedra saying to me in our first meeting, "People need to hear this!" Thank you for giving me the opportunity to spread the word about coupons and the Word of God.

Thanks to Josh Lease for helping me through this book writing process.

Thank you to our church family, and to Pastor Bob Yandian, for opening up your hearts to our family. Thank you for your warm embrace and the support all of you have shown to us personally and to 918 Coupon Queen. Truly, I could not have done this without such awesome encouragement and great teaching.

Storms are guaranteed to come in this life, but, praise God, we have a hand to hold as we walk through life's storms! If it were not for the circumstances we have walked through, I would have never learned this method, which is now feeding families all over our country.

However, all the coupons in the world do not compare with a real life relationship with Jesus Christ. I pray God is glorified not only in this book but in everything I do—to God be the glory!

Introduction

For such a long time it felt as if we were just getting by, holding out as long as we could before we had to make that grocery trip that was sure to take almost all of our money. We tried new things to save, from only eating cereal for dinner one week to trying to skip a week of grocery shopping just to save some extra money.

I also tried what felt like a million different moneymaking methods that only proved to *cost* us money. Would you believe at one time I tried selling tie-dyed curtains and pillows? I have had a lot of ideas, and each time I would push through them about halfway, and when the going got tough, I quit going.

I became really good at making up excuses about why this idea or that one did not work. My husband finally told me one day, "God has given you many great ideas, but you never stick with them long enough to see God bless them." Let's just say, 918 Coupon Queen is an idea that I actually stuck with. Through the twelve workshops in one month, the all-nighters searching for good deals to post, or the one hundredth retake for a news segment—we've stuck with it!

Everything we do here at www.918couponqueen.com is all about helping people feed their families. And I believe *God* is all about providing for you and your family. Coupons opened a door that we never knew was there, and it unleashed an amazing power to save money.

I encourage you to take some time to read over the story of Joseph (beginning in Genesis 37). Joseph went through horrible things in his life, one right after another. He ended up in Egypt before the Pharaoh, interpreting a dream. God used the dream to warn the Pharaoh that a famine was coming.

God used the dream to tell them that there would be seven years of abundance in Egypt, followed by seven years of severe famine. *"The abundance in the land will not be remembered, because the famine that follows it will be so severe"* (Genesis 41:31). Isn't it funny that we are so quick to forget how God has always provided for us when our circumstances change?

The people did listen, though, and they stockpiled their abundance, preparing for the time of famine. I do not believe this means we are to get all the food we can and pile it into our homes. Rather, I believe it shows God's provision. He cared enough to warn them about what was to come and tell them that He would provide for them.

Then, when the famine came, Egypt not only had enough food for its own people but also those in surrounding areas. Genesis 41:54 says, *"There was famine in all the other lands, but in the whole land of Egypt there was food."*

God spoke through Joseph's interpretation, the people obeyed, and the country had more than enough. Did you catch that? *More than enough.*

Aren't you glad we worship a God of "more than enough"? It may seem as though our country is going through famine; it may seem that way for you personally as well. Maybe you have lost your job or your spouse has lost his or hers; or maybe kids or life circumstances have caused your finances to be tight right now.

Remember, because Pharaoh listened to Joseph's interpretation and obeyed, even during the worst of famines, the entire country still had *plenty to eat.*

Let me say this: It does not matter what is going on in the world around you or what circumstance you are facing right now. God is bigger than your circumstances. God did not intend for you to live paycheck to paycheck, hoping and praying that you would be able to feed your family next week.

As believers, we are not a part of this economy; we operate in God's economy. Be encouraged today, and know if we listen and obey His Word, then even in the worst of famines, we will have "plenty to eat." You can be surrounded by famine on every side, but the famine will not touch you!

Therefore, I would venture to say that all this "coupon stuff" is more than just good timing; it's *God timing!*

"You will have plenty to eat, until you are full, and you will praise the name of the Lord your God, who has worked wonders for you" (Joel 2:26).

My Story

"The LORD will make you the head, not the tail. If you pay attention to the commands of the LORD your God that I give you this day and carefully follow them, you will always be at the top, never at the bottom" (Deuteronomy 28:13).

Chapter Highlights

- Life Happens
- The Tailspin from Faith to Advice
- Victory?
- The $600 Grocery Bill
- A New Day Dawns
- Learn to Rely on God
- Attacks Will Come
- God's Vision Takes Shape, Even Amid Challenges
- Beware Attacks from Unexpected Directions
- Healing Hearts

I found out I was pregnant with my first son in 2004. I was a preschool teacher at the time and knew that I would soon be staying at home with my baby.

The only problem was, I had no idea how that would be possible. My husband had a good job, but we just bought a new house and new car, so I knew that if I quit working, it would certainly throw our finances into a tailspin.

Six months into the pregnancy, I walked away from my job. I abandoned the thought of budgeting it out and planning every little detail—I simply walked away. I was tired, and my husband's nephew was living with us at the time, so I thought that it would benefit all of us if I were home.

I became Martha Stewart, Jr. The house was always clean, dinner was always made, and everything was perfect. That lasted for a while...and then life happened.

I became Martha Stewart, Jr. The house was always clean, dinner was always made, and everything was perfect. I began to read Proverbs 31 every day and seriously made it a goal to become the virtuous woman.

That lasted for a while...and then life happened.

Life happens

My son Elisha was born June 13, 2005. I had some complications during the delivery and had to have an emergency C-section. He was okay, though—which is what matters—and everything was great in the hospital.

That all changed, as it usually does, when we brought him home. He began to cry uncontrollably and for hours on end. I was trying to nurse him, but he just wasn't doing very well with that, either. We went a full 48 hours with no sleep. We took him to the doctor for his checkup and told her what was happening.

She suggested we supplement with formula. This was one of those Holy Spirit moments when, even through the chaos, I felt like I heard the Lord and we opted to use soy formula only. He slept for the first time in two days!

But I wanted to continue to breast-feed. So I kept trying and trying…and he kept screaming and screaming.

I don't know if it was lack of sleep or if I'm just slow, but we never thought it could be an allergy problem—after all, whose baby has allergies to *breast milk?*

We were in and out of the doctor's office for two months. I was put on a restricted diet, and still we got the same reaction—constant crying from one upset little boy.

Elisha had severe acid reflux. He was in pain constantly, and he vomited all the time. He also had eczema, so his precious baby skin was covered head to toe in rashes. Thankfully, we had an awesome doctor who kept studying, trying to find a solution.

"Viruses" and Allergy Testing

Over the next few months, we continued to deal with constant vomiting, rashes, and crying. When we introduced food, it only got worse. Test after test told us nothing. Within the first year of his life, we had taken Elisha to the hospital a total of thirteen times. And each time they told us it was only a virus.

The last time we took him, I pleaded with them, telling them that it was more than a virus. They inserted an IV into his head for hydration but still insisted that he had a virus and could not be admitted.

Then, we took the allergy test. It was a revelation and a confirmation of suspicions that had been growing for months.

My little boy's body had gone into reaction mode—he was now even reacting to food that he was not allergic to!

He didn't have viruses; he had *life-threatening* food allergies. He was allergic to wheat, soy, milk, eggs, casein, peanuts, tree nuts, tuna, garlic, chicken, turkey, and a few other odds and ends.

And worse, my little boy's body had gone into reaction mode—he was now even reacting to food that he was *not* allergic to!

The tailspin from faith to advice

Both my husband and I became Christians as children, and we grew up in the church. Both of us believed in divine healing and that it was as much for today as it was during biblical times. We knew how to believe for healing and how to stand on the Word of God.

Yet for some reason, in spite of all of this, our lives turned to chaos. I lost focus on God's promises, and I can still remember what that felt like. It was horrible. I prayed every day for healing, but I was panicking.

I began to listen to everyone's advice—whether they knew what they were talking about or not.

I took Elisha to a doctor who had no idea what he was doing regarding allergies of this magnitude. He had me buying more stuff for Elisha that, as it turned out, he was actually allergic to! (One time I took him into the office, and he even told me the problem was that Elisha was stubborn. He was only nine months old at the time!)

My life spun out of control. Now I was crying all the time, too, and I lived in a state of panic. I never knew what was going to make Elisha sick next, and I was extremely afraid that I would accidently give him something that would cause him to die from an allergic reaction.

Also, I held myself responsible for his allergies for a long time. During my pregnancy, I craved milk, cheese, and peanut butter. I ate them all the time. The guilt that I felt was nearly impossible to bear.

My husband was also deeply troubled by it. At the time, he was going to school and working *two* jobs to keep us afloat. Plus, deep inside, he began to think that he caused these issues because of his past life as an unbeliever.

Isn't it amazing what the enemy can put in our heads? Isn't it even more amazing that we actually *believe the lies?*

Victory?

After nearly a year of screaming and crying and the specter of life-threatening allergies, we went for counseling at our church. We were broken and hurt and scared for our son's life. We missed the mark somewhere and we knew it; it was just a matter of figuring out where that was.

An associate pastor met us that day, and what he told us changed our lives.

He told us we were believing God, but we were standing on the

He told us we were believing God, but we were standing on the Word after the incident had already occurred and not before—we were waiting until after Elisha was having a reaction before we went to God.

Word *after* the incident had already occurred and not before—we were waiting until after Elisha was having a reaction before we went to God.

He said we needed to change where we were putting the Word. We needed to speak the Word over Elisha all day long, whether there was a reaction or not. And, if he did react, we immediately quoted from Isaiah out loud, *"By His stripes we are healed!'* (Isaiah 53:5 NKJV) in Jesus name!"

We didn't ignore reality, throwing out his medicine or what we'd learned about his eating needs, acting as though his allergies didn't exist.

But we chose to believe the promises of life and healing in God's Word were true, no matter the circumstances.

We never had to take Elisha back to the hospital again for an allergic reaction. Our lives changed dramatically from that point on.

We knew we were the head and not the tail, above and not beneath (Deuteronomy 28:13) all along, but we had allowed ourselves to be pushed down and run over.

It was time to stand victorious!

The $600 grocery bill

We figured out fast that if he was going to eat, then we were not—we simply couldn't afford it.

As we were walking through this healing process, we began to learn what we could and could not feed our son. Soon, his grocery bill was nearly $600 a month! And he was only a year old!

We figured out fast that if he was going to eat, then we were not—we simply couldn't afford it.

We were buying him specialty organic food made in factories that couldn't share equipment with other types of food, which increased the prices of the food dramatically. Elisha's bread cost roughly $60.00 per month, his crackers ran about $15.00 a *week*, and his cookies also cost about $12.00 a week.

So, for three weeks, we did not buy groceries—unless it was for our son. We learned quickly that plan was not going to work; hunger is a strong motivator for change.

Then something happened that dramatically changed our lives. A man named Joe McGee spoke at our church. I remember listening to him and hearing him tell a story about all of his children and the amount of food they ate. He quickly referred to a promise in Joel 2:26 that said, *"You will have plenty to eat...and you will praise the name of the Lord your God, who has worked wonders for you."*

That one scripture changed our entire life.

I wrote that verse on 3x5 index cards all over my kitchen. Every time we walked into the kitchen, we saw that verse—God promised we'd have enough to eat.

A new day dawns

Three days after we heard Joe McGee speak, I walked into Walmart in search of specialty meat for Elisha. On top of that meat was a stack of coupons. I was blown away. I had not seen those coupons before.

For a long time, I had felt like the Holy Spirit was leading me to look into coupons, but I just couldn't figure out how to do it. I had

I walked out with about $150 worth of groceries for $19.00. It was life changing.

searched online and on eBay, but I still couldn't find anything solid that really seemed helpful.

I cut coupons out of the paper every Sunday, but, like many of you, I took them to the store only to find that the generic was cheaper. I will say, though, that I had cut them enough to know what was in the paper and what was not.

And those coupons on the meat in Walmart were *not* from our local paper.

I quickly hurried home and hit the net. I searched for hours trying to figure out where these coupons came from. I finally came upon a book written by Stephanie Nelson, *The Greatest Secrets of the Coupon Mom.*

I thought to myself, *If someone was willing to write a book about it, then there must be something more to coupons than I thought.*

I couldn't buy the book—we couldn't afford food for ourselves, let alone random books on the Internet—but I did check it out at the library. I memorized it, and that week, I hit one of the most expensive stores in our area armed with coupons and twenty bucks.

I didn't need to get a job, nor did I need my husband to pick up another job. As it turned out, all we needed were coupons!

I walked out with about $150 worth of groceries for $19.00. It was life changing.

If I can make it work here, it'll work anywhere

All of a sudden, I didn't need to get a job, nor did I need my husband to pick up another job. As it turned out, all we needed were coupons! Who would have thought?

The coupon technique wasn't all that easy for me to learn, though, because Tulsa, Oklahoma, was a little bit different than most cities throughout the country. I didn't have stores that tripled coupons—in fact, I only had a few stores that doubled coupons, so saving the kind of money I wanted was a bit tricky.

But, I kept at it, and I learned how to make the technique I'm going to teach you work for me in my city. I started learning the ins and outs of our local grocery stores and specialty stores.

This is part of what we'll learn together, because the techniques in this book are sound no matter where you live.

Spreading the word

I quickly realized I was saving at least $300 a month by using this coupon technique, and I knew I had to get the word out. Something inside of me told me that if it helped us this much, maybe it would help others, too.

I kept mentioning it to my friends, many of whom thought I was crazy. However, one of my friends suggested I teach a coupon workshop at a community center. It didn't take long before I was teaching all over our city. Not too long after that, I began a small website.

I asked my mom and sister to start e-mailing newspapers and news stations in town to see if they would be interested in interviewing me. As it turns out, they were! After my first newspaper interview, one of the

We realized that people wanted to learn how to save money, and many people were in the exact same boat my family and I were in—with more bills than salary and a desperate need to save money wherever possible.

founders of a new mommy site, www.918moms.com, contacted me. Soon after, I had a new name: "918 Coupon Queen." I began blogging on their website, and this book is the result of the momentum gained by working with the incredible people at www.918moms.com.

Within a matter of weeks, it was apparent to all of us that 918 Coupon Queen was a big deal. E-mails began to pour in, and we then began weekly news segments, radio appearances, and writing for a local Christian magazine. We realized that people wanted to learn how to save money, and many people were in the exact same boat my family and I were in—with more bills than salary and a desperate need to save money wherever possible.

Teach a woman to "fish" and she feeds her family for a lifetime

When I began to believe God for groceries, I went a step further. I didn't just believe God for a miracle every week just so we could eat. I believed God for a *continual method of increase* that would last much more than a week. I needed it to last a lifetime.

I didn't need someone bringing me fish; I needed to learn how to fish.

We're a spiritual people, a royal priesthood,[i] and we needed a supernatural solution to our problems.

Everyone wants a miracle check in their mailboxes—you know the stories of someone who opens his mailbox and there's this mystery check in there that comes in perfect timing to meet looming needs. Those are great to receive, and I'm not saying God doesn't do that, but it begs the question, "Did you learn anything lasting?"

My "check in the mail" was the stack of coupons I found in Walmart, and I thank God that it had a lasting impact on me and has armed me with something I can now give to others—a way of "fishing" that will help people meet their families' needs for years.

Anyone can tell you how to save money; anyone can tell you how to budget. And don't get me wrong—we need those things. But, those things are all in the natural world.

We're a spiritual people, a royal priesthood,[i] and we need a supernatural solution to our problems. We need the budgets, and we need the practical tips, but more than that, we need the Holy Spirit!

Learn to rely on God

During that period of time in our lives we learned how to save money and spend wisely, but, more importantly, we learned how to rely on God.

Remember, *"The thief comes only to steal and kill and destroy…"* (John 10:10). And let's just say that the thief is certainly good at his job.

> *Remember, "The thief comes only to steal and kill and destroy…."*

We had let him steal my family's health, our finances, our joy, our peace, and anything else he could get his hands on.

The good thing is that as we read the Bible, we learn more about our enemy—most importantly, that he's a defeated foe[ii] and is under our feet![iii]

But it doesn't always seem that way—especially when he's stealing more than your lunch money. We needed a dramatic change of perspective; we needed a realization about what was *true*, according to the Word.

So, after getting our heads put on straight with our counseling session, we decided that instead of letting the enemy steal from us, we would lay those things down as unto the Lord, knowing that we would get a return on them greater than we could ever imagine.

Do you think when the enemy hit our son with sickness that he realized we were going to believe God for healing and see him get healed?

Do you think when the enemy hit our finances that he knew we were going to stand on the Word and not only find a way to save money but would make a *business* out of it that would go nationwide?

Do you think he knew we would encourage others to save money and believe God while doing it?

I think it was a total surprise to him. And I'm glad to disappoint!

Attacks will come

Are you going to lie down and feel sorry for yourself, or are you going to stand on the promises in God's Word and put Satan right back under your feet where he belongs?

We suffer attacks all the time, but what God is looking for is our response. Are you going to lie down and feel sorry for yourself, or are you going to stand on the promises in God's Word and put Satan right back under your feet where he belongs?

I was tired of feeling sorry for myself; I was tired of blaming myself. I needed to know the Word, and I decided I was not going to roll over and let the enemy ruin my life or the lives of my children. That was over, and that was that!

For the last few years, we have been standing strong on the Word no matter what storms have come.

Right about the time I started thinking it was getting a bit too easy, we walked into another test. I found out I was pregnant again in 2007. Soon after my second son, Ethan, was born, we learned he had a heart murmur—and the doctor suspected something more. We went in immediately for testing.

We were all a little nervous after seeing all the equipment, but when we asked her if the test was something we needed to be concerned about, she said, "The only time you would need to be concerned is if I got up during the test and ran out of the room." She laughed while she said that, leading us to believe it wasn't likely to happen.

However, twenty minutes into the test, she got up and ran out the door. I was stunned, and some part of me knew that the enemy was testing our defenses again.

My second precious little boy had a heart condition. He had to keep going back for tests, and they told us that surgery might be our only option if Ethan's condition continued to worsen.

But we had learned our lesson the first go-round, and so this time we let that bad report go in one ear and out the other. Immediately, we were standing on God's Word, even as we stood in the back room waiting on the technician and the doctor to return.

We got out our healing scriptures and said them over our son. We didn't worry, we didn't stress out, and we just stood on the Word. Was it hard? Yes. Did I cry? Of course; this was my baby we were talking about.

But through the tears, we spoke the Word.

God's vision takes shape, even amid challenges

We kept going back for tests and following the directions the doctor had given us. The whole time, we just continued to believe that Ethan was healed—not that he *would be* healed but that he *was* healed.

In the middle of all this, I felt like God was beginning to give me a true vision for my business. I was starting to see things taking shape in a way that I had not before. I had just begun my partnership with www.918moms.com, and I felt like God was telling me not to just teach the method of couponing but also to encourage people with scripture and let others know that God cared about their groceries!

As long as we are here on the earth, we will be attacked until the Lord enforces His final victory. But again, what matters isn't the attack but our response.

You're holding the results of that vision in your hands, and you're about to learn that method!

My husband and I have grown in our confidence in the Word. We have learned what God has promised us, and it has become increasingly easier to recognize when the enemy attacks.

As long as we are here on the earth, we will be attacked until the Lord enforces His final victory. But again, what matters isn't the attack but our *response*.

Beware attacks from unexpected directions

We assumed we had dealt with all the attacks possible in the area of our kids' health. However, the next attack we were about to receive was one that I would never have expected. In fact, I would never have thought it even *possible.*

In the summer of 2008, we were called into the offices of our church. My husband had been a member there for sixteen years; I joined that church when we got married, nearly nine years ago at that point. We were very active in our church and had believed that our children would eventually go to school there when they were old enough.

When we got to the church offices, waiting outside the door of Elisha's normal classroom was a church employee; she had been waiting for us. Part of me was excited because I thought maybe we were going to record our testimony for the church to tell about what God had done in us and how wonderfully my oldest son was doing with his allergies.

I had often wondered what was hidden behind this beautiful set of glass doors in the hallway. As it turns out, it was an office—the Office of the Children's Pastor. We were greeted kindly and with great empathy, which made me realize I was not there to record a testimony.

Instead, we found out that my husband and I would no longer be able to attend church together. The children's pastor seemed very concerned about Elisha's food allergies and more concerned that he would react *while on church property.*

We felt the children's pastor's concern and have always felt that he grieved with us and sincerely cared about our family. However, the church *lawyers* feared a possible lawsuit could occur if Elisha were to react and we tried to hold them liable. I didn't quite understand what he meant until he said that anytime my son was on the grounds of the church, either my husband or

I had to be with him. He could not be alone...even in childcare. They didn't want the liability.

The pastor told us that they were open to suggestions and would be working towards a better solution, but for now, they asked us to abide by their requests to stay with our son at all times.

Liable not to change

As a former preschool teacher, I knew about the legal side of liability, especially when it concerned children, so neither my husband nor I had a problem complying with their request. We assumed it would not take long for them to come up with a better plan.

We became convinced that Satan was trying to get us out of church. And he was using my son's food allergies to do it.

However, a few months went by; my husband and I were no longer able to attend church together, I was no longer able to be involved in the women's groups or events, and we could not even attend the marriage workshops we had signed up for. We went from being at church five times a week to only being there two times a week for normal church services...and even then we were not able to be together.

We became convinced that Satan was trying to get us out of church. And he was using my son's food allergies to do it.

At first, the church staff came into the childcare rooms while we were in with our oldest son to give us updates or make sure we were doing okay. However, slowly, as we sat in those preschool rooms week after week, we realized no one was contacting us anymore. No one told us any changes were coming.

Basically, the policy of our sitting in the classroom with our oldest boy was indefinite.

We started making the necessary phone calls to figure out what was going on. Through several phone calls and e-mails over a three-week period, we learned that there were not going to be any changes.

I contacted a few family members in similar-sized churches and asked them about their policies concerning this issue. I made suggestions to our church, but those went ignored—in fact, when we did get an e-mail in return, it sounded almost robotic in tone.

All we were asking for was a ten-minute meeting to discuss our concerns. We e-mailed and we called, almost desperately trying to get a response. Both my husband and I knew what was happening—we were being ignored—and possibly even what was about to happen, but we just did not want to believe it.

Was our church really ignoring us? Were they trying to get us to *leave?*

The enemy was hurling thoughts into our head at the same time our hearts were breaking. I suddenly began to realize that we were fighting for my child's ability to attend church and our ability to attend it together.

Don't let the door hit you on the way out

Three months after we were asked to sit in Elisha's classroom, the church that we loved told us not to come back. In fact, they went so far as to say that if we came on the property again, it would be considered *trespassing.*

To make matters worse, only a few days after they removed us, *they started using the new methods that we had suggested.* The person in charge of this decision quickly informed us that it was a "privilege and not a right" to attend that church.

Who knew?

It was heartbreaking. And whether it was an attack or not didn't make it hurt any less. But we knew that what was important was our *response.* We didn't blame God, quit going to a church, or decide to feel sorry for ourselves.

Through the tears, we moved on.

As I said before, I grew up in the church. I have heard so many stories of people getting offended and never going to church again over matters that seem smaller. Many of these people get offended at church in general—or at God—because of something that one or two people did.

A handful of people were involved in our situation, and of those, only one made the fateful decision that hurt us so deeply. Did that mean then that we could hate that entire church? Did it mean we could bad-mouth that church and disregard the years of teaching that we had learned?

No. We had to respond as Jesus would have, turning the other cheek.

If we as believers are the Body of Christ and the Body of Christ is attached to the Head (which is Christ Himself), then how can you expect to be attached to the Head if you do not attach yourself to the Body (by going to church)?

If my husband and I were going to stay in line with Christ and raise our children up in a relationship with Christ—not a religion—then we had to get over it and move on.

Don't let people destroy your faith; your faith is not in people, it is in Christ Jesus. People make mistakes all the time—I do and you do, so why wouldn't church leaders be allowed to make a few mistakes?

Honestly, in our situation, I believe it was a grand miscommunication and an oversensitive team of lawyers. I know what happened to us was wrong on all accounts, but you know what? I cannot spend years dwelling on it; God is our vindicator, and He will mend what has been broken.

So what did we do? By the next week, we were sitting in a new church. Did it hurt? Yes, worse than any other hurt I have ever felt in my life. But, God has a purpose for every member of my family—including me—and we could not let the enemy take another moment of our lives away as we felt sorry for ourselves because of what they had done to us.

As Jesus said to the man who had been sitting by the pool of Bethesda for thirty-eight years, *"Pick up your mat and walk"* (John 5:8).

We picked up our mat, dusted off our feet, and walked ourselves into a new church—knowing that God could bless us just as much (if not more) in our new home than in our old. All that mattered is that we followed God.

And you know what I believe? God saw our response and honored it.

Healing hearts

About a month after we got the boot, Ethan had another heart test. We entered this test confident of what the results would be.

And instead of running out of the room, this time the doctor came in and said she could find *no evidence* of the former condition and that the heart murmur that was once there was barely noticeable!

The doctor confirmed what we knew all along: Ethan was healed!

It was by walking through those things that I can tell you assuredly today that we serve a very real God who cares about everything you do—even your groceries. I can tell you that the same God who gives life to the dead can give life to your finances!

If you want to get promoted in anything you are doing in your life, you have to learn how to respond according to the Word when the enemy starts trying to steal from you. God is looking for victors, not victims.

I'm writing these things to tell you this: You can let the enemy have the reins of your life, or you can stand up, put on the armor of God, take out the sword of the Spirit, and defeat the enemy!

We're going to spend most of this book looking at a way God showed me to not just receive "fish" from Him but a method you too can use to keep the enemy out of your finances and supply your family's needs. But first, let's look at some principles of Christianity I think are an important foundation.

God and Groceries

"My God shall supply all your need according to His riches in glory by Christ Jesus" (Philippians 4:19 NKJV).

Chapter Highlights

- God's Economy Isn't Tied to Ours
- God Will Do His Part; Will You?
- The Word is Alive!
- Watch What You Say
- Coupons Can Change Your Present, but Only God Can Change Your Future

Now that you know a little bit more about me, you are probably asking yourself, "What does God have to do with groceries? And where are the coupons?" Well, God has a lot to do with groceries, actually, and before we talk about coupons, I want to spend just a moment on a principle.

God says He has to do with our supplies when Paul writes in the Bible, *"My God shall supply all your need according to His riches in glory by Christ Jesus"* (Philippians 4:19 NKJV). I would say groceries are certainly a basic need. And since He says that He supplies our needs, well, that means He supplies our groceries.

So, it would only seem natural to me that if you were having a problem receiving your groceries, you would then contact the supplier, right? If the lights didn't come on when you flicked the switch, you'd call the supplier, the utility company.

God's economy never fluctuates or falters.

It's the same concept here. Obviously, you can apply this to anything, but since we're talking groceries, I'm just going to stick with that concept. If you are lacking in food, you need to contact your supplier.

That's what we did. We were lacking; we had hardly any food. So, we made sure we contacted the only One who could help us with that—our Supplier.

Rumors of doom and gloom for the economy are pretty common, and countries experience recessions and depressions and all kinds of negative economic times. As I write this book, the United States—and the world—economy is having troubles, but there's always good news: God's economy never fluctuates or falters.

God didn't say, "You will always have plenty to eat when the economy is up and everyone is making enough money." He said, *"You will have plenty to eat, until you are full"* (Joel 2:26). Period. That's what we need to understand. We, as believers, operate in a different economy.

Give and take

Our worldly economy says, "take" while our heavenly economy says, "give."

"Give, and it will be given to you. A good measure, pressed down, shaken together and running over, will be poured into your lap. For with the measure you use, it will be measured to you" (Luke 6:38).

That's not even normal return! Not only will we get blessed if we give, but we'll be abundantly blessed—that is a good deal! And, let me tell you that concept is just as true today as it was when Jesus said it. No matter what the economy looks like.

Let me also say to you one thing that our counselor told us when we went to seek help about healing. He said that if you do your part, God will do His part. Again, God is looking at your response.

Many times when people are hurting financially, the first thing they cut is their giving. Yet still they believe God for increase.

> *If you do your part, God will do His part. Again, God is looking at your response.*

But that is just not how God has set this thing up to work. Tithing is something God told us to do, and without it, we're actually being disobedient. Many people say, "I can't afford to tithe," but in God's reality, you can't afford not to.

Another problem is that many believers only tithe when they have money left over. But God has called us to give our firstfruits, not our last fruits. He said in Proverbs 3:9-10, *"Honor the LORD with your wealth, with the firstfruits of all your crops; then your barns will be filled to overflowing."*

Putting Him first in obedience

The firstfruits—the very first crops of the year—are symbolic. It means you're giving Him precedence, putting Him first, which is what Jesus was talking about when He said we are to seek the Kingdom of God first above all else, and live righteously, and trust God to give us everything we need—such as groceries.[iv]

That means when we get our money, our first check should be to the church—where you receive your spiritual food. This is the most fruitful soil you can plant in.

Some of you say, "I can't even afford to eat." Let me tell you this: God will not change His Word for you. He commands us to tithe, and when we do our part, God does His part—always.

If you are expecting a blessing from the Lord but are not willing to follow His commands, you will be waiting for a long time to come. You've got to obey.

Therefore, the first thing you need to be doing if you want financial provision—if you want groceries from your Supplier—is tithing.

Malachi 3:10 gives us an incredible promise: *"Bring the whole tithe into the storehouse, that there may be food in my house. Test me in this,' says the LORD Almighty, 'and see if I will not throw open the floodgates of heaven and pour out so much blessing that you will not have room enough for it.'"*

The living Word

As you are tithing, get out some index cards and start writing down scripture that applies to what you are believing God for. If you are believing for food, write Joel 2:26 on your card, the passage that changed my life so much: *"You will have plenty to eat…and you will praise the name of the Lord your God, who has worked wonders for you."*

Put cards with that on it in your kitchen—everywhere that makes you think of groceries. Every time you see it, say the verse *out loud.*

So many believers read the Bible yet never realize that it literally is *the Word of God.* Think about it this way: God created the whole universe with what? His words. He spoke and then it *was*—it wasn't, and then it was. Look through the first chapter of Genesis, and you'll see these words over and over again: *"And God said."*

That's right, God spoke and it happened.

"For the word of God is living and active," we read in Hebrews 4:12. It's not dead. It isn't for the past—it is for *right now,* and it is for your situation.

It's amazing that we have access to the very words of God, the very Word that gave life to this world. We have the ability to use the Word of God because He gave it to us, and He meant that we use it wisely. Applying it to your life for your needs is certainly part of the deal!

> *"For the word of God is living and active,"* we read in Hebrews 4:12. It's not dead. It isn't for the past—it is for right now, and it is for your situation.

The Word is your weapon against the enemy

Most people can agree that there's a devil out there and that he's bad news. Whether or not we understand who and what he is, most of us can agree he's the enemy.

But God hasn't left us defenseless: He has given us tools with which to resist the enemy and even told us *we'll win!*[iv]

Paul tells us about the lifestyle of living as a Christian, which has all the components of our walk with God as defenses against the enemy:

> *"Stand firm then, with the belt of truth buckled around your waist, with the breastplate of righteousness in place, and with your feet fitted with the readiness that comes from the gospel of peace. In addition to all this, take up the shield of faith, with which you can extinguish all the flaming arrows of the evil one. Take the helmet of salvation **and the sword of the Spirit, which is the word of God**"* (Ephesians 6:14-17 emphasis added).

He is telling us to take up our weapon—the Word! If the Bible were just a bunch of words on paper, then it wouldn't be a very effective weapon. But the Bible is actually *the sword,* the weapon with which we fight our stealing, killing, destroying enemy.

For examples of how this works, we have no further to look than to Jesus. When Satan tempted Jesus, how did He respond? He took out His sword—He spoke the very words of God and resisted the devil. And the devil *left.*

The power of our words

We as believers must understand the power of our words and the power of God's Word. As much as we can call life into being, we can also call death.

Walking around constantly saying, "I have no money," "I can't afford that," "I'm too sick," "I'm too tired to do that," and so forth is actually bringing those things into being in your life, whether you know it or not. In fact, whether you believe it or not, it doesn't matter—you create with your words.

This concept is an important spiritual law. If you speak life into your life, you will have it; but the reverse is also true. If you speak "death" into your life, you will have that as well.

What are you allowing to come out of your mouth? Worry, doubt, fear? I want to encourage you today to speak life.

What are you allowing to come out of your mouth? Worry, doubt, fear? I want to encourage you today to speak life.

If you need healing, then you need to start quoting God's Word regarding healing over your life. There are oodles of great books on healing and many audio messages on CD that read healing scriptures, and I'd strongly suggest getting some and then confessing those verses over your life.

When we started doing this, we did not see a miraculous change—my oldest son was still having allergic reactions. But what mattered was our *response*. When he reacted, we responded with the Word. And his allergic reactions got smaller and smaller and further and further apart.

Change your reality

If you need money, groceries, or really any good thing at all, begin to stand on the Word. Every time you open your empty cabinet, say out loud Joel 2:26, *"You will have plenty to eat, until you are full, and you will praise the name of the Lord your God, who worked wonders for you."*

You're not denying reality; we didn't stop giving our kid his medicine just because we believed he was healed. But we wanted the overriding reality of God's Word to replace the reality of our circumstances. When you quote the Word over your life, that's what you're doing.

It's time for us, as believers, to take a stand and make Satan wish he never messed with us!

Ask God to get in the mix

Anyone can give your budget a makeover, anyone can tell you how to get out of debt, and anyone can tell you to invest wisely. Those things are all great, and we need those things, but those things are in the natural, and what we *really* need is a dose of supernatural.

I can tell you how to save money with coupons, but if you're not making God an intimate part of this journey, this book is just another money-saving book of smart ideas that'll sit on your shelf but that won't change your life.

Instead, let it be a book that changes your life and does more than bring you extra money—let it teach you how to stand on God's Word and unleash God's blessing on your life and the life of your entire family!

These couponing techniques will alter your finances dramatically, but if you want long-lasting change, you must invite the Lord into the mix.

These couponing techniques will alter your finances dramatically, but if you want long-lasting change, you must invite the Lord into the mix. Ask for true guidance and wisdom, stand on the Word, and watch the mountains that have been sitting in the middle of your life for years fall before you. Unleash the power to save and be saved by the power!

Okay, now that you know my story and you understand these important principles, let's get to the coupons!

In the Beginning...

"If you are willing and obedient, you will eat the best from the land" (Isaiah 1:19).

Chapter Highlights:

- Defining Coupons
- Expiration Dates
- Knowing the Lingo
- Using www.918couponqueen.com
- Deciphering Matchups

Now that you have your armor on and understand the principles behind God's economy, let's march forward and talk money savings!

By the end of this book, you will be a coupon expert—and, more importantly, you will be a money-savings expert. The technique of couponing will cut your grocery bill by at least 50 percent, and for most, the actual savings are much greater than that. Hundreds of dollars will be coming right back to your wallet!

Let's start at the beginning, with defining coupons.

Manufacturer's Coupons

These are the most common coupons. They are directly from the manufacturer, meaning that the item's manufacturer will reimburse the store for the value of the coupon. You can find this form of coupon in the newspaper, on the Internet, on tear pads, catalinas, peelies, blinkies, in grocery circulars, and almost anywhere else you find coupons.

In 2008, over $334 billion in consumer incentives were distributed throughout the United States.

Marx Promotion Intelligence tracked over 251 billion manufacturer's coupons in 2008.

If manufacturers are going to the trouble of producing that many coupons and spending the money to track them, then there must be something to it.

In 2008, over $334 billion in consumer incentives were distributed throughout the United States.

Yes, the above statistic says *billion*.

That means that literally billions of dollars in savings are circulating throughout our country, but only a few realize it or take advantage of it. Instead, we read articles about turning down the thermostat, covering up with more blankets, and sealing our windows shut to save money.

While those things are good, and I've done them all, there is this amazing opportunity out there to save thousands—not just a few bucks or a few hundred bucks but *thousands*—of dollars every single year!

The average face value of a coupon has increased by 5.0 percent to $1.33!

We're not talking about $.25 coupons anymore: Many coupons are high dollar coupons and can also be doubled! Manufacturers want you to buy their products no matter what is going on in the economy, and coupons are the incentive to do so. Just think about it as financial stimulus for the grocery store!

Store Coupons

These coupons come from the stores themselves. Stores such as Walgreens or Target typically issue these types of coupons weekly either online, in their ad, or both. They are only redeemable at the store that issues them. Store coupons feature the store name or logo on the coupon itself.

These are sales in the form of coupons, so to speak. However, unlike sales, coupons bring many savings opportunities along with them! As more consumers look to coupons as a way to save money, more stores are responding with store coupons as a way to market the savings.

Want Walgreens coupons? Simply grab the weekly circular at the front of the store or in your Sunday newspaper. Walgreens has been known to place store coupons in nearly everything, from back-to-school promotions to coloring books!

These are only two examples of companies that use store coupons on a regular basis; tons of stores around the country have begun to use them, including specialty stores such as Whole Foods Market.

Companies do pay attention to what the consumer is interested in and carefully market according to our interests. Right now, we're all interested in saving money, and even people who have never clipped a coupon in their lives are breaking out the scissors! Companies are aware of this, and savings programs such as store coupons are a direct response to the desires of consumers like you and me.

Coupons are a direct response to the desires of consumers like you and me.

If you decide that you never want to clip a newspaper coupon, at the very least check out the store ad or website before you walk into a store! Just knowing the savings programs that your stores offer could save you hundreds of dollars!

Tear pads

These are manufacturer's coupons located on the shelf or display near the product itself. You simply tear the coupon off the tear pad and use it when you purchase the qualifying item.

Many times you'll find these on a big display showcasing a new product or a sales cycle. During back-to-school season, you'll find displays of school buses packed with back-to-school snacks, all of which are on sale. And more often than not, you'll see tear pads or brochures of coupons nearby.

Because it is a manufacturer's coupon, you can use it at any store, not just the store you found it in.

However, don't take the whole tear pad and make a mad dash for the nearest exit. Take a few and leave a few for those who need to buy that particular product that day.

Just recently, I walked through our local grocery store only to find $1.00 off coupons for SmartWater. I knew SmartWater was on sale at Target that week, so I took a few coupons from the tear pad over to Target and bought SmartWater for less than a quarter each!

Tear pads are ways for companies to get you to try their product while you are standing right there in the aisle, trying to make your decision. As you look to the left and to the right, scouring for that perfect bottle of barbeque sauce, you're more likely to try a new brand when you see a coupon dangling before it. It's a great way of direct marketing; we just have to learn how to use it to our advantage.

> *Tear pads are ways for companies to get you to try their product while you are standing right there in the aisle.*

Catalina

These coupons print out of a little machine after you check out. Catalina coupons are manufacturer's coupons issued at specific stores and are triggered by the product you're purchasing. The cashier usually hands these to you with your receipt, and they are typically blue or red.

Countless times I have seen these flying around the parking lot or lying in the grocery store trash cans—though I don't recommend crawling in after them. Although they do seem a bit cumbersome and look much like your receipt, they can actually be very valuable coupons! I recently received a Catalina coupon for a *free* gallon of milk because I had bought so many boxes of cereal.

Stores use Catalina coupons to encourage consumers to return to that particular store because they typically read, "Redeem at store XYZ." But remember, Catalina coupons are usually *manufacturer's* coupons. Many times, other stores will redeem these coupons because they are from the manufacturer. Of course, that totally depends on the store that you are in and what that store's policy is, which can vary widely from store to store.

> *The good news is that peelies can be used the next time you're at the store.*

Keep in mind that even though coupons are not cash, they will start feeling like cash because they literally will keep money in your pocket just by using them. Catalina coupons are often overlooked, but they can be a great source of savings.

Peelies

These are also manufacturer's coupons—ones that are stuck to the products. They peel off just like stickers, and you can use them when you check out with that particular item. You've probably gotten all the way home and unpacked your groceries only to discover a peelie coupon stuck to something. I know I have!

The good news is that peelies can be used the next time you're at the store. Don't just toss it to the side and think you've missed the opportunity; grab that coupon, stash it in your binder—you *do* have something to keep your coupons in, right?—and use it the next time you find a great deal!

Again, since these are manufacturer's coupons, you can use them at any store. But no, this does not mean you can rip off all the peelies that you find and take them down the street for a better deal.

I actually knew a woman who would go into the store in the evening and take all the peelies she could find. In my opinion, that steals from the other shoppers like you and me. Purchase your products and use your peelies; let's not take what does not belong to us.

You can use peelies at any store, though, which means if you get home with a peelie, you can use it anywhere—as long as it states that it is a manufacturer's coupon.

Sometimes you may have coupons for items and get to the store and find a peelie on the item. I've found that peelies tend to expire much later than traditional newspaper coupons, so I typically will use my newspaper coupon first and hold the peelie for a later purchase.

Blinkies

These are manufacturer's coupons in small boxes usually found in the cereal aisles. You take a coupon and another one immediately appears. These can be red, blue, or black and will sometimes feature blinking lights—thus the name.

Recently I walked into a store and found one of these machines that appeared to have a small TV screen attached to it. Very high tech for coupons.

You can go by and grab a few, but my rule still stays the same in this case as in the case of the other great coupon finds: Don't take all the coupons!

I've found these coupons to be great for double coupon days at certain stores (which we'll get into more later). Many times I'll see the boxes and I'll grab a few to hold onto for a later time when I know the products are going to be on sale or my store will be doubling coupons.

Internet Printable

This is certainly a type of coupon that is quickly gaining popularity. Most Internet printable coupons are manufacturer's coupons that can be redeemed at any store that takes Internet coupons.

Internet coupons are all the rage for several reasons. First, manufacturers can place Internet coupons directly on their website, meaning you are at the website on purpose and are more likely to only print the coupon if you are actually going to use it.

Internet coupons are also super convenient; you can print exactly what you want.

More importantly, it costs less to place a coupon online and keep it there than to put out mailers, inserts, or other printed coupons. Millions of Sunday paper inserts get thrown away each year, but Internet coupons are more of a direct marketing tactic—for those who look for them.

Internet coupons are also super convenient; you can print exactly what you want. You'll notice, however, that many sites limit you to two coupons. Sometimes, randomly, you'll see coupon websites like Coupons.com reset that midway through the month. (However, there is no way to know if they are reset unless you try to print them again at a later date, and you could waste quite a bit of time trying in vain.)

Many people ask if you need special software for getting Internet coupons. In my experience, the only software I have had to install when searching for Internet coupons is the Coupon Printer, which is simple and small.

If you have issues printing Internet coupons from a particular website, contact that website directly. Many times, they will send you the paper version via snail mail. In fact, here's a little confession: I've gotten way more copies of the paper version when reporting a problem than I ever would have with just the printable one on the website. Shhh!

Let's take a moment while we're on the topic to talk about where on the Internet you'll find these great coupons. First, I mention the hottest Internet printable coupons on a daily basis on www.918moms.com. This might be your only stop!

My website is a blog about the daily deals that I find or that our readers submit from all over the country. I blog about the newest deals and frequently post great Internet printable coupons to go along with them. Also, in our 918 Coupon Queen Forums, you'll find people chatting it up about the great deals they found at their local stores and the great coupons they have found as well!

So be sure to check out www.918couponqueen. com. first when hunting for Internet coupons!

So be sure to check out www.918couponqueen.com first when hunting for Internet coupons!

You can also visit Smartsource.com, Coupons.com, and Redplum.com for valuable Internet coupons. Many sites that offer Internet coupons only offer them for a short period of time, so it is best to print them when you see them. Sites like Coupons.com change their coupons monthly.

My favorite way to find coupons is by visiting the manufacturer's website. One of my son Elisha's favorite brands of allergy-free cookies is by Enjoy Life Foods. In fact, when I first found this company, I sat in the snack aisle and cried for joy. I did not think he would ever get to taste a cookie, and I was overjoyed when I discovered not only allergy-free cookies but allergy-free cookies that actually *tasted good!*

> *Insider's Tip: When you find a brand you love, visit the website directly. Chances are you'll find coupons!*

Since the Enjoy Life Foods brand is organic and a specialty food, the prices are a bit higher than your average box of Oreos. The good thing is that Enjoy Life Foods and many other specialty manufacturers offer great printable coupons directly from their websites! This is one of my favorite ways to find coupons!

Insider's Tip: When you find a brand you love, visit the website directly. Chances are you'll find coupons!

With the rise in Internet coupon popularity, coupon fraud has also been on the rise. We'll probably have coupon fraud cops before too long! (How would you like that for a career?)

There are stores around the country that have taken a hit and lost thousands of dollars due to coupon fraud. With that in mind, call your store before you shop and find out if they take Internet coupons. If they do, you're on the road to saving lots of money!

E-Coupons

This is the newest addition to the coupon world, a print coupon's high tech counterpart, if you will. E-coupons are literally making it easy for a generation on the go to save money.

E-coupons come on shopper loyalty cards that you can load with coupons and then take to the store, where the coupons are automatically deducted during your transaction. It's that simple.

Here are a few that I've found most useful:

- PGeSaver: This is a new program by Procter & Gamble that allows you to load your card with your Procter & Gamble coupons rather than clipping them from the newspaper. Procter & Gamble sends out a great coupon insert at the beginning of each month in your local Sunday paper. However, they also put these super coupons online for easy, clip-free access. Simply register, load, and swipe!

  E-coupons come on shopper loyalty cards that you can load with coupons and then take to the store.

- Shortcuts.com: AOL recently introduced Shortcuts.com as a savvy shopper's alternative to coupon clipping. Simply register your card, find the coupons you'd like to use, load them to the card, and head to the store.

- Cellfire: Cellfire.com is another great e-coupon site, and it allows you to access coupons via PC or even your cell phone! Yes, you can actually get a coupon on your cell phone! Simply show the cashier your text message at checkout. You can also load valuable coupons to your shopper's card for use at your favorite store, just like the companies listed previously. Cellfire isn't just for grocery coupons, though; you'll find deals for everything from flowers to restaurants to movie rentals!

- Upromise: The original e-saver. Hop on Upromise.com and register your shopper's card for valuable e-coupons and also to save money for your child's college education—what a deal! You can earn 1-3 percent back on your grocery purchases, 8 percent back from eating at preferred restaurants, and 1-25 percent back from shopping online through Upromise.com. Upromise.com is a great way to save money at the grocery store and give back to your family!

As e-coupons gain in popularity, you'll notice more and more grocery stores accepting them. If your store offers a shopper's loyalty card, definitely check out the sites above and see if your card is eligible for great savings.

Insider's Tip: Many times you can register each family member for a shopper's loyalty card and load each with coupons.

Insider's Tip: Many times you can register each family member for a shopper's loyalty card and load each with coupons. Also, don't let e-coupons take the place of real coupon clipping. While these sites do offer a lot of deals, they still do not come close to the deals offered in the Sunday morning newspaper or on online coupon websites.

Other Great Coupons

Register Rewards (RRs): Register Rewards are a type of Catalina coupon issued from Walgreens. In the weekly Walgreens ad, you will find sales such as "Buy Two for $5.00 and you'll get a $3.00 Register Reward."

After you purchase your items, a coupon will print out for $3.00 off *any item in the store* on your next visit! You can use Register Rewards like cash the next time you are in the store or in your next transaction.

Extra Care Bucks (ECBs): These are similar to the Walgreens Register Reward program except these are from CVS Pharmacy. In the ad, you will see sales that read, "Purchase $15.00 in Product XYZ and you'll earn $5.00 Extra Care Bucks."

You earn Extra Care Bucks with your qualifying purchase, and they're printed onto your receipt. You can then use them like cash on your next transaction or the next time you are in the store.

Cash Register Tap (CRTs): These are also at CVS Pharmacy. CRTs are coupons usually generated because of a specific purchase. They also print right onto your receipt. In some stores, you can actually scan your card into a machine to generate coupons.

Wine tags: Many states have wine tag coupons. These are coupons that are actually found on the wine bottles themselves. I mention them simply because they tend to be high-dollar coupons that are for things that you wouldn't expect. For example, it is not uncommon to find a wine tag for $2.00 off the purchase of meat or even $1.00 off the purchase of a bag of ice.

Before you think I'm advocating alcoholic purchases in the name of a good deal, think again. Most of these coupons *do not require a beverage purchase* even though they are hanging on wine bottles. However, these coupons can only be redeemed in states that sell wine in their grocery stores.

Insider's Tip: Read the coupon carefully and know your home market. You don't want to end up with a bunch of coupons that cannot be redeemed!

Insider's Tip: Read the coupon carefully and know your home market. You don't want to end up with a bunch of coupons that cannot be redeemed!

If you would rather not grab a coupon off a bottle of wine, you can purchase such coupons on eBay or other coupon sites. I never knew about wine tags until I discovered some on eBay. I had no idea what they were, so I bought some only to end up with a bag full of great coupons that could not be redeemed at any store in Oklahoma! If I wanted to save $2.00 on my meat, I'd have to drive to another state.... Tempting, but I think I'll pass.

Knowing the different types of coupons will help you find coupons for the products that you actually use. Now that you know the different types of coupons, let's discuss the anatomy of a coupon.

There are rules to couponing, and the expiration date is one of the biggest.

A word about expiration dates

Almost every coupon has an expiration date. That means that a store will no longer accept that coupon past the date listed. There are rules to couponing, and the expiration date is one of the biggest. Many stores are so sophisticated that their registers will beep if you try to use an expired coupon.

Make sure you are on top of your coupons every month and take out the ones that have expired. I hate being at a register with a cart full of products and a handful of expired coupons! It can be embarrassing, and you waste a lot of time hunting down all those products only to realize you won't be buying them (or you'll be paying way too much) since your coupons are long past due.

There are a few exceptions to this rule: First, overseas military bases can accept coupons up to six months past the expiration date. For more information on this, visit www.918couponqueen.com to learn about what to do with your old coupons.

There is also a small handful of stores throughout the country that will honor expired coupons. Just make sure you call and ask before you shop.

The expiration date is important: Don't ignore it!

Know the lingo

One coupon per purchase: This simply means you can have one manufacturer's coupon per item purchased. Makes sense, right? If you are purchasing five items, you can use five coupons.

Insider's Tip: For those of you who thought you could only use one coupon every time you shop, this may be news to you! You can actually use one coupon *per item*. When you want to buy three bags of chips and you have three coupons, you can use them all!

> *Insider's Tip: For those of you who thought you could only use one coupon every time you shop, this may be news to you! You can actually use one coupon per item.*

Now, keep in mind, this does not mean you can pile five coupons onto one item—it simply means if you have five items, use five coupons.

One coupon per transaction: (This could also be called "one per order.")You can only have one of this type of coupon per order or transaction. These are typically the "$25.00 off the purchase of $50.00 or more" type of coupons.

The reason why these are "one coupon per transaction" is that they do not want you stacking all those coupons on top of one another.

Insider's Tip: How do you use multiple "one per transaction" coupons? Simple! Divide your items into multiple transactions!

Insider's Tip: How do you use multiple "one per transaction" coupons? Simple! Divide your items into multiple transactions! It may be less convenient, but it's worth it to save money!

Recently, I had two coupons for saving $5.00 off the purchase of $50.00 or more, and I had $100 worth of products! So I separated my order into two transactions and was able to use one $5.00 off coupon with one order and the other $5.00 off coupon with the other order.

Sometimes getting a good deal just requires you to think outside the box.

Queen-sized matchups and shopping guides

Finding the sales, tracking down the coupons, and figuring out where to shop can get confusing and time-consuming. This is where coupon sites like my www.918couponqueen.com come into play. I do something called "matchups" on the site. I have wonderful volunteers who help me do this each week, and we actually take the sales flyers of various stores throughout the country and match them up with coupons to let you know your final price.

Insider's Tip: We've teamed up with some other coupon blogs that have offered their help as well. We take out our store circulars, log on to the Coupon Database, and whip out our binders to pair up great deals with great coupons to give you a shopping guide for the week!

Using our matchups each week will dramatically cut your couponing time. You can log on and print off the matchups if you'd like or sometimes even print off coupons that we've matched up with sales.

We offer many ways to help you find the deals you want—and find them fast! We update the site daily with new deals, offer forums for you to post your finds and ask questions, and offer a weekly devotional, restaurant deals, printable coupons and much more! And of course, it is all free!

Insider's Tip: We've teamed up with some other coupon blogs that have offered their help as well. We take out our store circulars, log on to the Coupon Database, and whip out our binders to pair up great deals with great coupons to give you a shopping guide for the week!

Simply log on www.918couponqueen.com and start saving money today!

I spent hours cutting coupons and matching up sales when I first began, only because I did not know anyone else who did this. It's amazing to have a group on board to help spread great deals to everyone. We know your time is valuable—I know I don't have much extra time to spare—and by using matchups you can cut your time in half...along with your grocery bill!

Deciphering matchups

For those of you who take advantage of the matchups offered on www.918couponqueen.com, you'll probably notice a few abbreviations. Let's take a moment and I'll bring you up to speed!

Most of the folks who put the matchups on our site try to let you know what insert the coupon came from. For example, Red Plum and Smart Source are two major coupon distributers. One of our matchups may look like this:

Brand Name Cereal $2.00

-$1/1 coupon SS 11/1/09

= $1.00 per box

This means the cereal is on sale for $2.00 per box, and if you use a "$1.00 off the purchase of one box" coupon found in the Smart Source insert that was distributed November 1, 2009, you'll get your box of cereal for only $1.00 per box.

Simple, right?

All you have to do is visit www.918couponqueen.com and click matchups and then find the store you need. It's that simple! You'll then know what coupon to use and where to use it!

Got a question? Feel free to ask questions on our forums! That's why they're there! Register for free and post your favorite deals and coupons or ask questions from the thousands of savvy shoppers on the site.

How awesome is it to be surrounded by so many folks wanting to save money just like you? And, if you are at the store and spot a great deal, feel free to post it—who knows, you may save thousands of people money from all across the country!

In the next chapter, I'd like to talk about something we all would love to do: Find hidden treasure. The great thing is, with couponing, you can find treasure all the time!

Finding Hidden Treasure

"The kingdom of heaven is like treasure hidden in a field. When a man found it, he hid it again, and then in his joy went and sold all he had and bought that field. Again, the kingdom of heaven is like a merchant looking for fine pearls. When he found one of great value, he went away and sold everything he had and bought it" (Matthew 13:44-46).

Chapter Highlights:

- How and Where to Find Coupons
- How Many Coupons to Collect
- How to Organize Coupons

Although this passage above is speaking about the Kingdom of Heaven, it provides a great illustration about hidden treasure. Think of couponing this way—like a hunt for hidden treasure.

> *Before you get a second job, cut the cable, and sell your other car. I dare you to try couponing.*

Do you like the idea of finding hidden treasure? I think we all like the idea of finding something wonderful and unexpected.

Before you get a second job, cut the cable, and sell your other car. I dare you to try couponing. Join me in the hunt for hidden treasure!

Everyone's situation is different, and you may have to cut back and scale down. But I encourage you to try this method first—I've done the rest, and there are drawbacks.

At first I felt silly using coupons; I felt like it was something my grandmother would have done. But maybe it's time we learned a few lessons from our grandmothers! Trust me, it is *much* cooler to use coupons than to bounce a check!

But as wonderful as coupons are, I often get asked one very important question: "How do I find coupons for products I *actually* use?"

This is a tough dilemma, especially for those who eat organic or specialty food. But the truth is most of the food my family eats is organic or allergy-free—so we've had to get creative to find coupons. Read on, and I'll show you how, too!

Where to find printed coupons

Here's a great tip: ask family and friends who usually throw away coupons to save them for you. Many of my family members still do this today—and they're related to the Coupon Queen!

When I began to coupon, I also began calling my friends and my family members who I knew probably threw the coupons away each week. I even called my dad, who actually uses coupons a lot, and each week he would pass along what he didn't use to me. Now, I find coupons in my mailbox all the time!

Put on your blog, Facebook and/or Twitter that you are all about couponing and ask others to send them to you. Trust me: Soon, you'll end up with tons of coupons just by spreading the word!

Insider's Tip: Check out places such as retirement homes where papers are delivered but food is also provided. Many of these residents do not use the coupons in the paper, and they will save them for you. My grandmother's retirement center is my main source of newspaper coupons! Ask around and see if you can put a basket at the reception desk or in the lobby where the residents can drop off their coupons after they read their papers.

Insider's Tip: Check out places such as retirement homes where papers are delivered but food is also provided. Many of these residents do not use the coupons in the paper, and they will save them for you. My grandmother's retirement center is my main source of newspaper coupons!

Check out stores on Monday to purchase Sunday papers at a discounted price—or better, for free. You may have to ask around for these, but many small gas stations will offer discounts. You'll also find many mom and pop convenience stores will offer discounts on Monday or if you purchase multiple papers. Typically, big chains donate their papers to schools and/or local libraries, but smaller stores will just throw them away. But the bottom line is that it never hurts to ask!

Where to find coupons online

You can also order coupons online from many different websites including eBay, since different parts of the country receive different coupons. You can type in something simple like, "Capri Sun Coupons" and buy them for extra low prices—and sometimes free shipping.

> *Insider's Tip: Look for the expiration date of the coupon—you don't want to order coupons that expire next week!*

I have found many useful coupons on eBay, especially since my oldest son has a very specific diet. I have been able to purchase tons of coupons for organic products that I rarely see otherwise. For those of you who are brand loyal, let eBay become your new best friend!

Make sure you are purchasing manufacturer's coupons. *Technically,* you cannot "buy" coupons; you are merely paying for the time a person put into finding and clipping those coupons. Be sure to check out that person's feedback.

Insider's Tip: Look for the expiration date of the coupon—you don't want to order coupons that expire next week!

Remember, if you purchase $20.00 worth of coupons for only $.99 then take those to a store that doubles coupons—then you've actually saved $40.00!

I tell people it's not really worth the bother to buy Internet coupons online; they're too easily altered and, if you own a computer—which you probably do since you're buying them online—you can probably print them yourself without the hassle of ordering them online.

Check out the manufacturer website to sign up for coupons or print them right off the website. Most major manufacturers offer coupons directly from their website. All you have to do is click and print! This is also a great option if you are loyal to a certain brand or if you see a good sale that you'd like to pair with a coupon. Simply checking out manufacturers' websites can land you tons of Internet coupons!

Don't know who the manufacturer is? Simply Google the name of the product or, if you have the product in hand, turn it over—you'll probably find a website!

Remember, if you purchase $20.00 worth of coupons for only $.99 then take those to a store that doubles coupons—then you've actually saved $40.00!

While you're there...

Sign up for e-newsletters while you are there; they are great sources for coupons. Just be sure to provide an e-mail address other than your primary address. Otherwise, you'll quickly find your inbox full of newsletters from companies all over the country. I prefer using a free e-mail resource such as Hotmail, Yahoo, or Google for a dedicated coupon e-mail address.

Honey and vinegar

E-mail the manufacturer to either praise or complain—and make sure to include your address! Even if the form you're filling out does not ask for an address, make sure to include one just in case. Also, it doesn't matter if you've already printed off the coupons from their site—it never hurts to ask for more!

Legitimate complaints or suggestions will usually get you coupons for free products. However, I strongly recommend you only do that if you have a real problem. Praise goes much further than complaints! Most companies will go the extra mile to make the customer happy, but a customer who is already happy makes the company (remember, every company is made of real people) feel good—and they'll reward you for that.

One of the biggest problems with e-mail is that it can be so anonymous. You can e-mail someone or a company and tell them exactly what you think of them and their product knowing full well that you will never see that person. I have felt wronged by a company and sent an e-mail to complain, but I think it's important even then to remember to be civil and polite. Besides, I'm pretty sure Jesus can read your e-mails.

And always remember that no matter how big or small the company is, there is a human being on the other end of that e-mail. If you really want to earn brownie points with a company and get the best deals, be legit and be kind.

By phone

Call the manufacturer to praise or complain about their products. This is very similar to the suggestion above regarding e-mail, and the same rules still apply. However, you can call the companies even though you have already e-mailed them and signed up for their newsletters. And, you can ask not only for coupons but *samples* as well!

When you have that person-to-person encounter on the phone, you are able to inquire about the company or products and savings methods. When you are talking to a company, be sure to ask when you can call back—some companies will let you call back every 14-30 days to ask for more coupons and/or samples!

I called a baby formula company recently and not only did the lady I talk to send me coupons, she also gave me the dates for the next six months so I could call back and ask for more! On top of that, it was a discounted store brand formula—even they offered coupons!

Just this week, I used coupons for *$2.00* off a pop (or soda) purchase (including two-liter bottles)! How did I get those? By calling the manufacturer! Those are high-dollar and extremely valuable coupons, and calling the manufacturer is the best way to score those kinds of coupons! And, again, make sure to ask when you can call back!

Store coupons

Be sure to find out if your store offers store coupons. Companies like Target and Whole Foods offer store coupons on a regular basis. Target lists them on Supertarget.com, and Whole Foods provides them in their newsletter titled, *The Whole Deal,* which is available at the front of the store. Many grocery stores also offer store coupons, so do a little digging and see what your favorite store offers.

Insider's Tip: Log onto the 918 Coupon Queen Forums on www.918coupon queen.com and ask around to find what stores in your area offer store coupons frequently and also where to find them.

Insider's Tip: Log onto the 918 Coupon Queen Forums on www.918couponqueen.com and ask around to find what stores in your area offer store coupons frequently and also where to find them.

Magazines

All You magazine, which costs about $3.00 at Walmart is filled with coupons! Visit <u>Allyou.com</u> for two free issues! This magazine is great for coupons and money-saving articles. You're likely to find coupons in this magazine that you won't find in others.

Women's magazines are great resources for high value coupons. Women are a target audience for companies, as we tend to make most of the household shopping decisions. Before you toss out your used magazines, check them for coupons!

Swap Box

Here's another great idea: Try trading with friends and acquaintances to get the coupons you need. Make a coupon box for schools, day cares, churches, etc. All you have to do is place new coupons in the box whenever you take one out.

I recently taught a coupon workshop at my son's preschool, and after the workshop, the teachers gathered together and used a filing cabinet to sort their coupons and create a swap box. During the week, the teachers and moms could go to the box and take what they needed and replace the coupons they took with new ones. Then, once a month, a teacher went through the box and removed expired coupons.

Let's say that you don't have kids; you can put coupons for kid products in a swap box for people who do. They in turn might have products you need for your yard or pets. By pooling your resources, you can help others get what they need and find the coupons you need too!

What a great way to get the coupons you need and share coupons instead of just tossing them!

All aboard the coupon train!

Now, you're probably thinking, *What in the world is a coupon train?* Simple—a coupon train is like a chain letter for coupons!

Coupons are regional, so one part of the country may receive something that your city just doesn't get; this is where the train comes in. You can join coupon trains to trade coupons with other people *all across the country.*

We've introduced these to www.918couponqueen.com. All you'll have to do is visit our forums, sign up for a train, and when you get an envelope full of coupons in the mail, simply take what you need and replace those coupons with some extras from your stash, then send it on to the next person!

I used this method for a long time. I loved the day my envelope arrived—it was full of coupons for products that I actually used and needed to purchase.

Many times sales vary widely from state to state and store to store, so even though one thing might have been a great deal for someone else in another state, it wasn't a great deal for me. So, I was able to pass along coupons, spreading the great deals throughout the country!

> *Insider's Tip: Typically, you don't want too many folks on the coupon train or it may take weeks to get your coupons. Try just starting with family and friends!*

Insider's Tip: Typically, you don't want too many folks on the coupon train or it may take weeks to get your coupons. Try just starting with family and friends!

Coupon Swap Parties

Here at www.918couponqueen.com, we've been holding coupon swap parties for a while. We find a great spot like a favorite coffee shop, invite folks from all over the city to join us, and remind them to bring their coupons, scissors, and organizers!

We spend hours chatting about deals, clipping coupons, and showing off our stash! It's a great way to meet people, and it takes the swap box to the next level!

Insider's Tip: Just as with the box or the train, trade for what you will use and share what you don't need at coupon swap parties!

This is a great way to not only grab coupons but also meet folks who share the same money-saving desire as you! You can hold these parties at libraries, restaurants, and even retailers—in fact, we recently held a very successful coupon swap party at a Whole Foods Market! We showcased organic food and had a great time!

Many of the ladies on our site are new moms, and our parties are great ways for them to get together and swap diaper coupons. If you use a product and need coupons for that product, consider a coupon swap.

Insider's Tip: Just as with the box or the train, trade for what you will use and share what you don't need at coupon swap parties!

A few tips for a successful swap

1. Coordinate: Someone has to take the lead on these things and coordinate. Even if you've never done one before, you

can still use common sense to follow the rest of these tips and have fun figuring them out!

2. RSVP: Make sure to have everyone register so you can plan accordingly. This is especially important if you have to order food. There's nothing worse than ordering food for fifty and having only ten show up. Also, the response will tell you if your location is suitable or not. Preferably, make the RSVP an e-mail address and then the week of the swap you can e-mail all attendees a reminder. There are all kinds of easy automated invite and reminder sites!

3. Location: Pick a location with plenty of space for coupon cutting and chatting. We've learned from experience that wide-open spaces make it hard for us to hear one another. Also, we need plenty of trash cans and recycle bins for all those extra clippings. You'll want a place that can accommodate your guests *and* the huge piles of coupons and organizers. Think big!

> *Insider's Tip:*
> *Scrapbooking places often make the best coupon swap locations—they are already prepared for cutting!*

Insider's Tip: Scrapbooking places often make the best coupon swap locations—they are already prepared for cutting!

4. Snacks: At www.918couponqueen.com we have been able to provide the snacks and drinks for our coupon swappers. However, you don't have to! Ask everyone to bring a snack and feast potluck style! In fact, that can be your admission price: one snack per person! I personally have always felt

that a workshop or swap party is not complete without food. I love sitting around snacking and cutting coupons; it makes for a great time, and your guests will enjoy it too—especially if your party lasts several hours and people start getting hungry. However, if you are meeting at a restaurant and need to order trays of food, you may want to charge a small fee per person for your swap party. Some places even charge a fee for using their spaces—make sure to check out these costs first!

5. Advertise: Ask the managers of your location if you can advertise on their bulletin board or window. Get it out there on your personal social networking forums—and on www.918couponqueen.com! Advertise anywhere people are with whom you'd like to swap coupons. If there are stores in your city that are big for couponers, ask if you can put a flyer at the register or on display. Spread the word at your church too—coupon swaps are great for church groups! Get a buzz going around and ask your family and friends to come: Even if they have never clipped coupons before, this is a great place to start. We always attract newbies at our coupon swaps, and many times, people just sitting in the restaurant come over to see what is going on—new recruits!

Remember: Most of all, just have fun. This is not a high-stress party; it's a time to fellowship and have a great time!

6. Relax and have fun! Remember you're not teaching a class! This is a coupon swap, so get down and get your hands dirty! Create a relaxed atmosphere, break out the name tags, and have a few drawings for coupon organizers or subscriptions to *All You* magazine. Remember: Most of

all, just have fun. This is not a high-stress party; it's a time to fellowship and have a great time!

Other places to find coupons

Remember alternative places to find coupons—Smartsource coupons, Catalina coupons, etc.—and if possible, grab another city's paper when you can. Coupons can vary widely from one city to the next, even if they're relatively close!

Don't underestimate the newspaper; it is a fantastic source of manufacturer's coupons! They change every single week. Recently, our paper had over $3,000 worth of coupons!

Check out McDonalds, hotels, coffee shops, and other places for folks reading papers but leaving coupons behind. Their trash is your treasure. Of course, I would make sure these establishments are okay with your gleaning used newspapers, but most just throw them away. It's worth checking out if you can!

You might think this is a little extreme, but don't write off recycle bins! Jump in and score all those leftover coupons! You are still recycling—just drop off your newspaper and reach in for coupons. In our city, you can find recycle bins at libraries and even at Walmart. I see folks bring in newspapers by the truckload, so when you stop by to throw your newspapers in the bin, look in and see if there are any coupons sitting on top.

918 Coupon Queen Disclaimer: Okay, maybe I don't recommend literally jumping into the bin, but you can lift the lid, and if you can reach some coupons, then go for it! Otherwise, I wouldn't jump into a huge trash bin if I were you. But, then again, it depends on how good the coupons are!

If you get your newspaper delivered, ask your delivery person what they do with the extra coupons. Many times, they'll pass along the hidden treasures to you! I found a delivery woman who was throwing her coupons away each week; she ended up giving me 28 inserts! I couldn't believe it!

Asking around doesn't hurt a bit; offer your delivery person some hot chocolate and find out what he or she is doing with all those juicy coupons. Some newspaper companies may require them to return the coupons, but from what I've found, most just throw them away!

How many coupons do you really need?

Now that you've gotten some great tips for *getting* coupons, let's take a moment to talk about how many you can actually use.

That simply depends on how much you want to stockpile or have room for (more on this later). When you learn how to get your item at its lowest price, you'll then want to stock up on that item so you don't have to buy it full price later. Since you can use one manufacturer's coupon per item, you're going to need more than one coupon to stock up.

I have heard several couponers say that it is best to have one coupon per person in the family, per item, but if you are going to stock up for a couple months, it may take more than that.

Insider's Tip: To cut multiple coupons, the best way is to gather all like inserts together, staple them in the top corners, and take a pair of really sharp scissors and cut them all at the same time. I can cut about 15 inserts at one time using this method.

Cutting coupons

When you start to get going, finding your coupons and gathering them from friends, you're going to have *a lot of coupons.* You'll find that you've got stacks and stacks of printed fliers and newspaper inserts. So how do you deal with all that?

Insider's Tip: To cut multiple coupons, the best way is to gather all like inserts together, staple them in the top corners, and take a pair of really sharp scissors and cut them *all at the same time.* I can cut about 15 inserts at one time using this method.

You can also cut coupons with a paper cutter or wrapping paper cutter. Since I don't have room for a real paper cutter, the sharp scissor method works best for me. As for the wrapping paper cutter, it's quick but you can only cut one insert at a time, so I found out quickly that I do not have the patience for that!

Your other option is to store the coupons in their original condition in some kind of file folder or cabinet. Then, cut them out as you need them. This method is difficult for me because every store has tons of unadvertised sales going on each week. I've found that I end up at the store with only half of my coupons cut out—and sitting in an aisle with two kids and a pair of scissors is not ideal to me!

Some stores literally have thousands of unadvertised sales. I actually cut out all the coupons I am *definitely* going to use and also those that I may use if the items are on sale. Leave in the insert the stuff you don't use or need and the crazy, off-the-wall coupons for items that you know you wouldn't buy even if they were free!

Organizing coupons

Okay, so now you've got them cut out. What's next? What do you do with all these flimsy little pieces of paper?

Insider's Tip: I store all of my coupons in a three-ring binder and use baseball card dividers to hold the coupons. It's great because I can have twelve different coupons on one page, and I fold them so I can typically see the item and expiration date.

Insider's Tip: I store all of my coupons in a three-ring binder and use baseball card dividers to hold the coupons. It's great because I can have twelve different coupons on one page, and I fold them so I can typically see the item and expiration date.

Binders are also handy because you can put official coupon policy info in them, just in case you need it.

I organize my coupons in sections such as the following:

- Frozen Products
- Dairy Products
- Meat Products
- Drinks
- Personal Care Products
- Pet Products
- Child Products
- Snack Foods
- Cereals
- Cleaning Products
- Organic Products
- Store Coupons

You can also buy dividers for your binder that have pockets on them; those pockets can easily hold store circulars. You can attach a pencil bag to the front of your binder—put a calculator, pen, and a pair of scissors in there in case you need them!

Organize your binder in a way that makes sense to you. The methods I am telling you about in this book are methods that have worked well for me. I am not an excessively organized person, so I need something super easy and quick that I will keep up with, especially since I also have small children.

The key is organizing your coupons in a way that makes sense to you and lets you find them while you're in the store! If you can't find your coupons, you won't use them!

The key is organizing your coupons in a way that makes sense to you *and lets you find them while you're in the store!* If you can't find your coupons, you won't use them!

Essentially, you can use anything to hold your coupons, such as a shoe boxes, photo organizers, or even recipe boxes. If it works for you, then that is all that matters.

I like the binder method best because it is easily portable. I have probably $30 invested in mine, when you count the price of the baseball card dividers. They're relatively inexpensive, widely available, and you can have as many as you want! Let's just say I have a lot of pages.

If you'd like to organize even more, you can create different binders for different things. Some couponers have one binder for food items and one binder for non-food items, or you can have different ones for different stores.

You can also use a purse-size organizer. Those are the ones you see most often, and in fact, I actually used to sell them in my classes. The problem with those is that once you start collecting tons of coupons, they'll all get lost in that little organizer. They typically have twelve little pockets, but they fit right into your purse or diaper bag—great when you're getting started!

I used to recommend that you file your coupons in your binder and then take the coupons that you know you're going to use on your next store trip out and put them into the purse-size organizer. I then realized I was hauling *two* kids and *two* organizers into the store—it just didn't go well, to say the least. You can always tell when I've been in the store; I leave one trail of lost coupons and another trail of Cheerios.

The bottom line is to find a method that will be easy for you to use. I'd hate for you to get frustrated and just give up because of unorganized coupons!

The Business of Coupons

"Blessed is the man who finds wisdom, the man who gains understanding" (Proverbs 3:13).

Chapter Highlights

- The Marketing of Coupons
- Real vs. Fake
- Coupons: Denied

I don't know about you, but I can always use more wisdom. Coupon cutting was that for me: a wise way of saving money and helping my family...while staying with my boys instead of heading into the workforce.

So let's take a look at the business of coupons and gain a little coupon wisdom!

Big business

As I mentioned before, coupons are a billion-dollar business used for marketing products. Say a company is coming out with a new product or a different flavor. How do they get that product into your home? Offer a coupon.

What's the first thing you think of when you go buy a product? Price. Chances are if you are reading this book, then saving money is a priority for you. Companies know that—especially during rough economic times.

So, when they want to get a product into your house, they know they have to offer a good deal, and that is exactly what they do. In fact, some of the best coupons are issued when a company comes out with a new product.

Their purpose is for you to buy that product and like it enough that you will *continue to buy that product* even if there isn't a coupon for it. They want you to be brand loyal. And, for most consumers, it works.

Typically, a company will place their newest, best, and even most expensive product on the coupon itself.

Typically, a company will place their newest, best, and even most expensive product on the coupon itself. Even though the coupon states clearly, "$1.00 off any Brand XYZ product," your eyes are drawn to the picture. Therefore, the average consumer will purchase whatever product is in the picture even if it is the most expensive.

The average person only gets one newspaper. So even though your family buys three boxes of cereal a week, most people only have one coupon for that cereal. You'll go into the store and buy the one box you have a coupon for, but you'll also go ahead and buy the other boxes you need—with or without a coupon.

They've got you! But you don't have to play their game!

If a company wants business, offering sales and coupons is truly the way to go. There's a golden opportunity in front of you to take this big-business sales tactic and use it to your advantage. Instead of saving a few dollars here and there, let's look on at how to save *hundreds* by using this coupon business to its fullest extent!

Win-win situation?

So, if that's how the companies make money, what about the stores? Lots of marketing is going on at the store level as well. For example, look at the front page of your grocery circular/ad. Those items are called Loss Leaders.

What that means is that the store actually takes a *loss* on those items to bring you into the store. Chances are you'll grab those items and then you'll grab other items that you need as you grab the sale items.

Just think about it: When you see BBQ sauce for $.99 you think, *Wow—that's great!* Then you hit the store only to realize you need hamburgers to put the BBQ sauce on. And then since you're buying hamburgers, you might as well get hamburger buns, and since you are buying buns, you might as well get tomatoes and onions too! And since you are buying tomatoes and onions, you might as well get drinks...and so on and so on. Pretty soon, your $.99 BBQ sauce cost you $200!

In some stores, they actually move their Loss Leaders to hard-to-find spots, causing the consumer to have to walk past tons of other products on the way to grab that one sale item. It is a little tricky, but the tactic works well. Stores will also impose limits on Loss Leaders such as two or four per person—that is an easy way to discover a true Loss Leader; they have limits.

Remember, companies want your brand loyalty, so they issue a coupon; stores want you in the door, so they offer a good sale. You want to save money—everyone can be happy!

> *Remember, companies want you brand loyal, so they issue a coupon; stores want you in the door, so they offer a good sale. You want to save money—everyone can be happy!*

The trick to being a smart shopper is being aware of these strategies and learning how to use them to your benefit.

Who pays?

This then typically leads to the question, "How does the store make money when coupons are used?"

When a manufacturer issues a coupon and it is redeemed at the store, the store gets reimbursed by the manufacturer—plus a small amount to cover postage. The store does get their money back when you use coupons.

Several things work to the manufacturers' benefit:

1. Consumers are buying the product, which creates a demand at the store. More products are then ordered and possibly given an even better spot on the shelf—or even better, their own display.

2. Consumers like the product (and as we discussed earlier, they are going to come back for more), so even though the manufacturer may have lost $1.00, they may possibly gain many thousands in the long run. Even more so if

the consumer becomes brand loyal and continues to buy all of its products, the manufacturer has long-lasting repeat business.

3. Coupon blogs are becoming a huge marketing force these days. Companies offering good deals know to check out the coupon bloggers, like me, because we see thousands of visits every single day. Therefore, if they've issued a good coupon/deal, chances are bloggers around the country are blogging about it and the manufacturer has now increased the audience by hundreds of thousands— all without doing anything more than offering a coupon!

Some companies are so aware of the new force of "mommy bloggers" that they are offering free products—and in some cases money—so the blogger will post about her great deal, coupon, and product. In these cases, typically, the blogger only accepts if it is indeed a good deal worth spreading. Consumers are listening to other consumers much more than they ever have before.

According to Marx Promotion Intelligence, Freestanding Inserts (coupon inserts) reach almost 70 million homes on a weekly basis.

Those are just the inserts; just think about all the Internet coupons! We're literally talking *billions of dollars* in coupons each year! If you thought couponing was just a fad, please realize this is a huge industry making stores and manufacturers *big money* each year!

This is also why stores and companies get so upset when fraudulent coupons arise. Let's talk about how to avoid buying, finding, or using fake coupons.

Real vs. fake

First, let me say that using fraudulent coupons knowingly is a crime, and you can be *arrested* for it—wow! It also costs the store money, and if they lose enough money, they will change their coupon policy.

This is why so many stores stopped using Internet coupons. Now, some stores will accept them and others won't.

Really, I do not believe tons of people are out to use fake coupons, and there are not as many out as you might think. Going out on a limb here, sometimes I think stores overreact and make snap decisions rather than bothering to see if they are actually fake or not.

Recently, a few fake coupons surfaced out of a particular city. To stop people from trying to use Internet coupons from that city, some stores decided that *all* Internet coupons from that city were fake. In reality, only a few of them might have been fake, but they banned them all.

> *It's every respectable couponer's responsibility to help stop the spread and use of fake coupons—it's in our own best interests!*

The more you coupon, the more you will realize what the real thing actually looks like. Once you know that, you'll easily be able to decipher real from fake. Yet I think it's every respectable couponer's responsibility to help stop the spread and use of fake coupons—it's in our own best interests!

Think about it like this: When you read the Word of God daily and meditate on His promises, His will, and His ways, it's not hard to see when the enemy is at work. You know the real thing—God's ways—and when an imitation comes your way, you can quickly identify it and put it "under your feet" where it belongs.

How to spot the frauds

Here are a few common characteristics of fraudulent coupons:

1. Many times fraudulent coupons are for "FREE" products. There are companies that do distribute coupons for totally free products; however, it's usually a part of a big marketing promotion that can be easily located on the company's website or newsletter. Sometimes the company may send you a coupon for a free product when you have called the manufacturer about a defect or other issue.

   Overall, companies do not issue free product coupons without reason. In my classes, I often tell folks if they receive a coupon for a "free product," they should make sure they can trace it back to the manufacturer directly.

   In one of my workshops recently, a woman mentioned that a certain store was no longer accepting Internet coupons. She simply wanted to make sure people knew that the store might hassle them if they went in with their coupons. That struck me as a bit odd, since I shop at that particular store all the time. I asked her what happened and she said she tried to use two coupons and they were denied even though she had used them before. She then told me the coupons were for free products.

   It just so happened she had those coupons with her at the class, and I asked to see them—sure enough, they were fake. Both were for free products, and neither had expiration dates or correct redemption language on the coupons.

2. Fraudulent coupons tend to be .pdf files or some other type of file that can be easily altered. Typically, someone may have taken a legitimate coupon and then altered the amount of that coupon to something outrageous like FREE or $10.00 off the purchase of *one* bottle of water.

   These can be a bit hard to figure out if they are legit or not—the main way to tell is if you can trace it back to the manufacturer's website. If it's on the manufacturer's website, then chances are it is legit; otherwise, be wary. If it's too good to be true, it probably is.

3. Many fraudulent coupons are also distributed via e-mail. Someone creates it and sends it, giving it the viral effect of being passed along from e-mail to e-mail until it has spread throughout the country. Again, if you can't trace it back to the manufacturer's website or if it is not an official e-mail or newsletter from the manufacturer, then chances are it is fake.

Insider's Tip: Use common sense when checking out coupons. If it's outrageous or can't be traced back to the manufacturer, chances are good it's fake. Beware!

Insider's Tip: Use common sense when checking out coupons. If it's outrageous or can't be traced back to the manufacturer, chances are good it's fake. Beware!

I received a coupon in an e-mail once for a free milkshake from a local restaurant. I looked at the coupon and saw a few weird items: the first was that the address on the coupon was email@email.com. The second was that it was a free large milkshake that typically runs about $3.99 each, which seemed like a very high value coupon. It is not common for a restaurant to simply issue a free coupon for that high of a value without requiring another purchase.

Since I see legit coupons all day long, seeing those things did raise a red flag; however, because I got it from a friend who was reliable and because I started to see it on other coupon sites, I went ahead and posted the coupon. It didn't take long until the head of the corporation e-mailed me and told me it was fake—after nearly 2,000 people had seen the coupon.

4. Counterfeit coupons also tend to have no expiration date. I actually found a fraudulent coupon that had no expiration date, but on the bottom of the coupon it stated, "Redeem Quickly." Interesting.

   Most coupons do have expiration dates on them. Occasionally someone will give me a coupon from years ago for $.05 off a bar of soap and it has no expiration date. It is a legit coupon and I'm tempted to use one just to see the reaction I would get. But nowadays, almost all coupons have an expiration date.

   If you contact a manufacturer directly to report a complaint or inquire about coupons on occasion, they will sometimes send you coupons that do not expire. But if you received them directly from the manufacturer, you can be confident they're legit.

5. Stores and companies typically become aware of fake coupons quickly and thus issue warnings to store employees telling them not to accept that type of coupon. But this sometimes causes employees to stop accepting coupons altogether. In those cases, it is best to call a manager to

resolve the issue. Remember, coupon policies can change and vary greatly by store.

I will go out on a limb here and say that the majority of the time your coupons will be legit. However, if you do use a coupon and a store lets you know that it was fraudulent, don't worry—just apologize and put your items back or continue with your purchase.

Many times stores that have had major issues with coupon fraud will take a very strong stance against coupon usage. That is why it is very important that we, as couponers, make sure we are using valid coupons.

So the question is, "What happens when you know you are using valid coupons and the store still won't accept them?"

Coupons: Denied

When you arrive at the checkout ready for the world to see your unbelievable deals, what do you do when the clerk says to you, "I'm sorry but we can't take *those* coupons?"

Everyone is looking at you, and that makes it seem as though you are holding some kind of bomb in your hands that may explode if put into their registers.

So now what are you going to do? Scream, yell, and throw your Chex Mix? We'd all like to do that. But, in the real world, we must play nice. So here's what you do when your coupons get denied.

1. **Make sure you're not wrong.** There's nothing worse than fighting to the death for your coupon only to discover you were trying to use an expired coupon or that you did not read the coupon thoroughly. For example, a cashier told me that a woman had come into her store and tried to

stack five manufacturer's coupons onto two boxes of cereal. The woman was irate, called a manager over, and made sure everyone knew she was very upset. She misunderstood the policy and was literally fighting with the employees—even though she was wrong!

Mistakes happen, but let's remember we are representing Christ. And quite honestly, yelling and screaming over $.25 doesn't make sense to me.

2. **Check the coupon policy.** Make sure you can use Internet coupons at that store, check the fine print, and so forth. If possible, print the official coupon policy and carry it with you in your binder. Sometimes employees do not even know the store policy, so having a copy comes in handy. You can simply point it out to them. Stores like Walmart post their coupon policy online, but for other stores, just send them an e-mail and see if you can get an official coupon policy. Smaller grocery chains may not have one; in those cases simply ask your questions and get the name of the person you spoke to.

3. **Be nice. Very nice.** Even if the temptation hits you to get hysterical, keep your cool. People do not respond well to screaming; it's just in our nature. Nice goes a long way.

4. **Always, always ask to speak to a manager.** Do not take the cashier's word for it; ask politely to speak to a manager. Just like many employees don't know their store's policies, general coupon training often isn't mandatory—they may just not know what to do with you.

A manager can set the record straight—whether that be good or bad. Sometimes managers have the right to change the policy if they feel that it should be changed.

However, it does not mean that every single store in that chain has changed. You may be better off just going to another store.

5. **Get your money back if you've cashed out.** If the situation persists, ask them to put your items back and get your money back. Then, call/e-mail the corporate office to let them know what happened. You do not have to purchase those items, you can easily put them back and walk out of the store.

Be the bigger person

Once you really start couponing, chances are you may run into a few issues with your coupons. Most of the time it is a simple misunderstanding that is quickly resolved. However, there are those rare occasions when the world falls apart right in front of you. That's okay—just be the bigger person, grab your binder, and walk out the door.

> *Insider's Tip: Chances are, there's another store down the street that would just love to have your business.*

Insider's Tip: Chances are, there's another store down the street that would just love to have your business.

In my workshops, I teach the official coupon policies to date. However, if Manager Joe decides he doesn't want to take your coupons, that's up to him. You'll have to take that up with corporate. Typically stores are not supposed to change their coupon policies on a whim, and calling the corporate offices can get things right back on track.

I get a lot of e-mails from folks who have had a coupon issue at a store. While I do want to know if policies have changed and I do want to hear your stories, I do not work for a store so I cannot properly handle the issue for you. If you want to see real change or if you think you were done wrong, please contact the manager and/or the corporate offices. They do listen to customers!

If you want to see real change or if you think you were done wrong, please contact the manager and/or the corporate offices. They do listen to customers!

This also works if you want your store's coupon policy changed and you've never had an issue there. One of our 918 Coupon Princesses was able to share her thoughts about offering double coupon days to a manager of a grocery store nearby. And guess what—he listened!

In fact, he called over some of his cashiers to watch her check out at the register and make sure they could handle the coupons properly.

A good word can go a long way!

Proverbs 15:31-32 says, *"He who listens to a life-giving rebuke will be at home among the wise. He who ignores discipline despises himself, but whoever heeds correction gains understanding."*

It's all about how you speak to someone. If someone sends me an e-mail offering a suggestion while also telling me how much she has enjoyed my workshops, website, or whatever, I am more apt to listen than if someone were to send me an e-mail telling me everything I do wrong and how to fix it.

By nature, I am a glass half empty person. I've had to fight that my entire life. I can walk into someplace beautiful and newly redone, and my eyes will only see what is wrong with it. It works out great when I need to see something that is wrong and fix it, but most people do not want to hear about what they do wrong—they want to hear about what they do right.

God won't promote and bless griping, negative people who don't watch what they confess. For those of us with a "glass half empty" personality type, we must constantly be aware to be kind and thankful—even when things are going wrong. It takes being constantly aware of this and making a valid effort at changing the way you think and speak.

If you want changes to happen at stores or with companies, it's all in how you present it. Compliments go much further than yelling, and if you'll keep a level head, you should have no trouble weathering the occasional coupon mistake!

In the next chapter, we're going to get to something I know you've been waiting for—13 great ways to cut your grocery budget in half! I can't wait to clue you in on these great tips!

13 Ways to Cut Your Grocery Bill in Half

"But the fruit of the Spirit is love, joy, peace, patience, kindness, goodness, faithfulness, gentleness and self-control. Against such things there is no law" (Galatians 5:22-23).

Chapter Highlights:

- Organize
- Use Coupons at the Right Time
- Keeping Track
- Stockpiling
- Shop Smart
- Combine Coupons
- Changing Brands

- Changing Stores
- Know the Lingo
- Fine Print
- Multiple Transactions
- Unadvertised Sales
- Meat

Now that you have a basic understanding of couponing, let's move on to cutting your bill by 50-80 percent! That means if you spend $1,000 per month, you could *easily* cut that to only $500 per month by using the coupon techniques below.

You've just found enough income to equal a part-time job! And guess what? It won't take you away from your family!

Insider's Tip: Take some time each week to plan your grocery trip, cut your coupons, and visit the matchups on www.918coupon queen.com.

#1—Organization

The key to all of this is organization—stay organized, and you'll succeed. Get confused, and you'll waste time and money.

Insider's Tip: Take some time each week to plan your grocery trip, cut your coupons, and visit the matchups on www.918couponqueen.com.

It will take some careful planning, organizing of coupons, and some extra time to get started. Give yourself the time to do it right! Do not put time constraints on yourself as you get started, or you will be frustrated quickly.

I usually tell new couponers to give themselves one or two hours per week to cut, organize, and plan, but it may take you longer. That's okay—learning the system is worth it!

Once you catch on, it will come naturally. I can plan my trip, cut my coupons, and be out the door in thirty minutes or less now, and I've got two little boys vying for my attention!

You'll also learn to plan ahead. For instance, say I have a lot of things going on in the next few weeks and I know I will not be able to do a lot of the grocery shopping. So, this week I will sit down and plan my coupon trip ahead of time.

In that time, I'll clip my coupons, go through the ads, print off matchups from www.918couponqueen.com, and make my lists.

Insider's Tip: When you get your list down, stick to it—remember you are only at the store for *exactly* what you came for! Limit impulse purchases but be sure to bring all your coupons in case you spot an amazing unadvertised sale!

After planning my shopping trip, I'll go to four stores for the best deals—all within one mile of each other. The result? I'll spend about $150 (keep in mind this will last two to three weeks for our family of four) and save nearly $300.

The planning takes me about forty-five minutes, and I saved my family $300! *That* is what makes all this worth it.

Insider's Tip: When you get your list down, stick to it—remember you are only at the store for exactly what you came for! Limit impulse purchases but be sure to bring all your coupons in case you spot an amazing unadvertised sale!

Remember, couponing does take a bit of self-control. You won't be grabbing everything you see; no more quick trips that turn into $100 trips, and no more buying whatever you feel like buying whenever you feel like buying it.

Remember, couponing does take a bit of self-control. You won't be grabbing everything you see; no more quick trips that turn into $100 trips, and no more buying whatever you feel like buying whenever you feel like buying it.

What's the good news? YOU SAVE A TON OF MONEY!

You might be thinking that you don't know how you'll find that kind of self-control. But the neat thing is, you actually already have it—you just have to use it!

In Galatians 5:22-23 Paul writes, *"But the fruit of the Spirit is love, joy, peace, patience, kindness, goodness, faithfulness, gentleness and self-control. Against such things there is no law."*

If impulse shopping is something you have a hard time with, write these verses, Galatians 5:22-23, on your coupon binder. Then confess the Word and shop smart!

#2—Timing

If you want to save the mega money, you have to learn *when* and *where* to use your coupons.

Insider's Tip: One of the biggest tricks to saving money on your groceries is using a coupon when your item is at its lowest price.

That means you must wait until your item *is on sale* before you use your coupon! Now, you'll double the savings! This takes both discipline and shrewd observation skills, but the savings are well worth it.

A specialty store in our area actually offers discounts for buying by the case, too. So, you can wait until your item is on sale, use coupons to purchase your items, buy *a case* of it, and save an extra 10 percent. With that deal, I'm using three different savings methods at one time! Now *that's* good timing!

Insider's Tip: One of the biggest tricks to saving money on your groceries is using a coupon when your item is at its lowest price.

Did you know certain items such as chips, salsa, BBQ sauce, and so forth go on sale during a certain time of the year? Did you also know new products and/or flavors are not only likely to go on sale but also likely to have coupons? If not, have I got news for you: Timing on these things is very important if you're going to maximize your savings.

I want to introduce you to my friends—"sales cycles." They occur throughout the year, and you need to make friends with them, too. If you do, you can really cash in if you combine the great sales with your coupons. This takes a little planning, but being ready for a sales cycle can really slash your grocery bill!

Here's a quick summary of the yearly grocery sales cycles:

January	Diet foods, Super Bowl snack foods, oatmeal, chili, soups, pop.
February	Canned food, hot foods such as waffles and oatmeal, dog food, chocolate, Chinese food.

March	Frozen food: dinners, waffles, ice cream, veggies, etc. Easter items go on sale too (depending on when the holiday falls), such as eggs, ham, etc.
April	Other times in the year, you'll get your Easter items here: eggs, ham, candy, sugar, cookies; Jewish foods; also, Earth Day promotions for organic foods.
May	Summer kickoff begins: BBQ items, hot dogs, hamburgers, condiments, produce, grilling items such as charcoal, outdoor items such as sunscreen, allergy medication, etc.
June	National Dairy Month: milk, eggs, cheese, butter, yogurt, ice cream, etc. Father's Day promotions, including BBQ items such as charcoal, BBQ sauce, grilling meats, etc.
July	Even better BBQ sales: grilling meats, condiments, chips, bread products, produce, ice cream, baked beans, etc.
August	Back to School: breakfast bars, cereals, Kellogg's promotions, Lunchables, juice boxes, snack items, peanut butter, jelly, and school supplies.
September	Back to School Promotions continue; pasta, pasta sauce, tomatoes, and baby items such as diapers, creams, feeding products, etc.
October	Candy, chocolate, pumpkins, and fall baking items.

November Thanksgiving items: turkeys, stuffing, sweet potatoes, pies, and marshmallows. Also, hot cocoa, oatmeal, soups.

December Holiday baking/dinner items: frozen rolls, green beans, potatoes, cream soups, ham, butter, flour, bread, pie crusts.

The above list lets you know when the items are most likely on sale. You'll be more likely to find those rock-bottom prices during that time, so it's a great time to stock up. So, how big is your pantry?

But if you really want to save money, you'll have to learn how much your items cost at their absolute lowest.

#3—Keep Track

Most of us buy hundreds of items in a month, making it nearly impossible to track the prices of all those items. But if you really want to save money, you'll have to learn how much your items cost at their absolute *lowest*.

We, as consumers, tend to buy many of the same things each week, and we already know the average price of the products we buy, such as our $3.99 box of cereal. But what's the *lowest* price of that cereal?

You may know your favorite box of cereal is $3.99 per box, so when you see it on sale for only $2.99, you automatically think that's the best deal. But what if I told you that your cereal could go as low as *$1.50?* Now your good deal doesn't look so good.

So how will you know how low your cereal can go?

Insider's Tip: To find out how low it'll go, simply begin to track the price of your cereal over the next few weeks. You can do it for as many as twelve weeks, because most sales cycles occur every twelve weeks.

Insider's Tip: To find out how low it'll go, simply begin to track the price of your cereal over the next few weeks. You can do it for as many as twelve weeks, because most sales cycles occur every twelve weeks.

So, if your favorite cereal is on sale this week, it will likely be on sale again within twelve weeks. What is important is that you realize when a good sale actually is. Sometimes stores may cut the prices back a bit but it's not really a *great* sale. And because we only have a ballpark figure in our minds, we can't recognize the difference between a good sale and a great sale.

Place a small chart in your coupon binder at the very front so you can start keeping track. You can make a simple Excel chart or other spreadsheet if you'd like, or you can simply track the prices on a piece of paper. Each time you enter the store, write down the price of your item, and keep at it for twelve weeks.

I wouldn't suggest you track all 200 items that you buy in one month—that's way too many and it could get you frustrated. So start small and take the top ten or twenty items you purchase and begin to track just those prices.

You will begin to see the price of your favorite box of cereal go up and down. Maybe the lowest price is $2.99. Or maybe it's $1.99.

What do you do when you find your lowest price? *Use your coupons!*

That's right—wait until you find the lowest price and *then* use your coupon. When your cereal is $1.99 and you use your $1.00 off coupon, your cereal is only $.99! Or, if your store doubles coupons, your cereal may be FREE!

Look at these examples:

Wait until you find the lowest price and then use your coupon.

Normal Price:
Kellogg's Frosted Flakes $2.99 per box
- $.50/1 manufacturer's coupon from the newspaper
= $2.49 per box

Sale Price:
Kellogg's Frosted Flakes $2.49 per box
-$.50/1 manufacturers coupon from the newspaper
= $1.99 per box

918 Coupon Queen Deal:
Kellogg's Frosted Flakes $1.99 per box (lowest price)
-.50/1 Manufacturer's coupon (doubled)
=.99 per box

By buying your box of cereal at the rock bottom price with your coupon, you saved $2.00! And that can really add up if you buy several boxes every month!

But, now that you have gotten your favorite box of cereal for next to nothing, how are you going to take advantage of that deal so you don't pay full price next time? The answer, stock up!

Remember, most sales do work in the twelve-week sales cycle.

#4—Stockpiling

Ah, sweet music to any couponer's ear. Essentially, stockpiling just means when you get your item at the lowest price after your sale and coupon, then you've got to stock up on that item until it goes on sale again. If you have been tracking your prices, then you probably have a good idea when your item will be on sale again. Remember, most sales do work in the twelve-week sales cycle.

During those yearly and twelve-week sales cycles, you'll not only see low prices at the store, but you'll also see tons of *coupons* for those items as well.

Insider's Tip: Coupons and sales do tend to follow the seasonal trends. By realizing that, you'll know when it's time to stock up and on what.

For example, September is a great month for baby sales. Therefore, more coupons for baby products can be found during that month, which also means September may be the best time to stock up on all things baby. Be sure to plan your family accordingly! Just kidding!

Stockpiling can be a sticky topic among couponers. So, let me say a few things: I've seen a fellow coupon guru's pictures of large rooms dedicated entirely to her stockpile. I've also seen garages, patios, and so forth stocked full of food, deodorant, and pretty much anything you would ever need if the world decided to fall apart tomorrow and you were put in charge of feeding all of the human beings left on the planet.

The philosophy of stockpiling is this: If you find items free or really cheap, then you'll want to stock up on them then rather than having to come back and pay full price when you need them again.

However, sale cycles come around every twelve weeks; this means that typically you need not stock up beyond twelve weeks because another good sale will come along. Unless, of course, it is a seasonal item such as BBQ sauce, apple pies, salsa, soup, or what have you.

And then there are those rare occasions when you'll see deals that you've never seen before, and those call for extreme stock up measures. Recently, after coupons I was able to purchase my shampoo and conditioner for *free!* I went ahead and bought enough for an entire *year* so I wouldn't have to go back later and buy more shampoo. I'm ready for a whole year, and I did not pay anything! Now *that* took a lot of coupons—and a lot of storage space.

Stockpiling vs. hoarding

Stockpiling has to be done in consideration of how much your pantry will hold and also how much you actually need. I recently watched a news video of a fellow couponer in another city. She was leading the cameras through her garage, which was stocked floor-to-ceiling with feminine products, shampoos, soaps, pens, paper, canned goods—you name it. Just about everything you could ever want was inside that garage, like she was ready to weather the end of the world.

> *Stockpiling is a great method of saving money—in fact, it's one of the biggest—but there is a difference between stockpiling and hoarding.*

The problem? She already had plenty for her family, and each week she was back at the store for more. How many razors does one woman need? Besides that, she has little children—I seriously doubt she even shaves her legs that often!

I'm afraid that this woman has gone beyond frugal into obsessive.

Read what one of our users wrote: "I've seen a lot of hoarding lately...I'm sad to see moms sharing deals they got and then there's nothing left for the rest of us!"

Stockpiling is a great method of saving money—in fact, it's one of the biggest—but there is a difference between stockpiling and hoarding. No one can tell you how much is too much; that depends on the individual situation. But use your own God-given judgment and *common sense,* especially if you already have stashes of those products at home.

Insider's Tip: Make sure you are actually *using* the items you're stocking. I keep a running list of stockpile items in my coupon binder (on your pantry door is good too) so I can see when I am running low and what I need to keep an eye out for.

If you are running low on pasta sauce, make a note on your stockpile list, consult your chart, and for the next couple weeks, keep watch for good sales and coupons. If you see a deal you can't refuse but you

Insider's Tip: Make sure you are actually using the items you're stocking up on. I keep a running list of stockpile items in my coupon binder (on your pantry door is good too) so I can see when I am running low and what I need to keep an eye out for.

simply *do not need*, bless someone else with it so we can all have "plenty to eat" (Joel 2:26). This is where swap boxes and hopping on www.918couponqueen.com to blog about your find comes in handy— share the wealth!

Remember, if you stockpile too much pasta and never eat it, chances are in a few years, you'll find that some little whiskered "buddies" have been nibbling your idle hoard.

When stockpiling, it is important to remember these tips:

> *Remember, if you stockpile too much pasta and never eat it, chances are in a few years, you'll find that some little whiskered "buddies" have been nibbling your idle hoard.*

- Do not purchase an item that will expire soon unless you can store it properly.
- Invest in a good freezer. You will be able to stockpile meats and other items effectively, and the cost of the freezer will be well paid back in money you save!
- The expiration date does not matter in most cases if the food is properly frozen. (This doesn't mean you should eat something frozen in 1984.)
- Stockpile what you will *actually use* and replenish it as the stock dwindles.
- Organize your pantry and label accordingly so you can easily see your stockpile.
- Keep track of your stockpile.
- Think creatively. Use an extra closet, build a shelf above the washer and dryer, or place a four-shelf unit in your

Insider's Tip: Look through the ads and find the deals by matching up the sales with your coupon. Or, take the easy way out and look at our matchups on www.918coupon queen.com! Let us match up your ads with coupons so you can just print and go!

garage to hold your stockpile. If you have to remodel your home to hold your stash, it's probably too big.

Your stockpile will be a key to savings and—when done in moderation—a true blessing to your family!

#5—Shop by using your ads and coupons

You know those grocery ads you get every week and toss out? Good news: Those actually are worth something! Now that we know all about Loss Leaders, here is how we use them to our advantage.

Insider's Tip: Look through the ads and find the deals by matching up the sales with your coupon. Or, take the easy way out and look at our matchups on www.918couponqueen.com! Let us match up your ads with coupons so you can just print and go!

Do this for a while and you'll quickly realize that the "Everyday Low Price Store" may not be the best deal after all... Traditional grocery stores offer sales and discounts that other stores simply do not offer.

Sometimes it is worth checking out stores other than the biggest names. Or, if you price match (more on that later), you'll need to look through the ads to find the best deals. The weekly sales ads will soon become your best friends when you learn how to use them to your advantage.

By combining a sale with a coupon, you're likely to create rock bottom prices!

Change the way you shop, not the way you live

If you haven't noticed yet, this requires changing the way you shop. You must plan your grocery trip around your ads, coupons, and stockpile.

If you have just stocked up on all things BBQ because it's the middle of the summer and hamburgers are cheap, then use a little imagination and make some fabulous meat dishes!

Some people think that if you use coupons and sales, then you are limited to having to cook those items, but that's not the case. We are simply changing the method of shopping—not necessarily the products, just the method.

If you haven't noticed yet, this requires changing the way you shop. You must plan your grocery trip around your ads, coupons, and stockpile.

Remember, by taking a little time to organize your shopping trip, you will literally shave hundreds of dollars off your grocery bill.

After you get a good stockpile going, you will actually be buying products to replace your stockpile as you use it, and you'll be buying perishable items like milk and eggs, too.

Recently, things got really busy. I taught nine workshops in one month and couldn't get to the grocery store. However, we had a great stockpile and hardly noticed that we had not gone grocery shopping in nearly a month! I was able to cook dinners and make lunches—all out of what I had already stocked up on!

Matching the ads with coupons will really make a difference in how you shop. I can already hear you asking, "Does this mean I have to shop at twenty stores a week?"

Not necessarily. However, shopping a different store or a few different stores each week will likely increase your chances of saving money. Make sure to factor in gas, though; I once drove a total of forty-five minutes to save $4.00. Lesson learned.

Remember, by taking a little time to organize your shopping trip, you will literally shave hundreds of dollars off your grocery bill.

If you would rather shop at only one store, just make sure to use all the savings policies that store offers. For example, many stores will price match. Simply take in your ads, and many will match their competitors' prices. You can also use coupons with these items for an even better deal!

Shopping different stores lets you take advantage of store coupons or frequent shopper cards that cannot be used anywhere else. Therefore, it may be worth an extra trip. I have literally saved hundreds of dollars at these types of stores— those were way better deals than if I would have just settled for price matching.

You'll want to have multiple sets of coupons so that you can purchase multiple products at the absolute lowest price possible, and then you can stockpile those items. The best way to get that low price is by matching up your coupons with a great sale. So, when it's BBQ time, grab your ketchup coupon and match it up with a $.99 sale. You just stocked up on ketchup for only $.25 per bottle—now *that's* a good deal!

#6—Combining coupons:

A manufacturer's coupon is redeemed from the manufacturer itself; therefore you may only use one per product. A store coupon is redeemed (or considered a loss) by the actual store; you can only use one of these per product as well. These may be two coupons for identical products, but the redemption process is totally different.

> *Insider's Tip: In most cases, you can combine a store coupon with a manufacturer's coupon (this is called "stacking").*

Insider's Tip: In most cases, you can combine a store coupon with a manufacturer's coupon (this is called "stacking").

It looks something like this:

Kellogg's Frosted Mini-Wheats Cereal on sale for $2.00 per box

-$1/1 Manufacturer's coupon (possibly found on the Internet or in the newspaper)

-$1/1 Store Coupon (possibly found on the store's website or in the ad)

= FREE Kellogg's Mini-Wheats Cereal

Store coupons are amazing for this purpose. Oftentimes, it can make stores that may typically seem overpriced actually *cheaper* than other "lower priced" stores. You can use a manufacturer's coupon and store coupon on the same item at the same time because the coupons are redeemed two totally different ways!

Store coupons are simply "store sales" put in coupon form; many times these could also be considered Loss Leaders, as they are simply a way of drawing you into the store. (But, as smart shoppers, you know that you are only going into the store for *exactly what you came there for*—right?) Many stores also offer store coupons that do not expire for several weeks; this gives you time to find more coupons to match up with the store coupons.

Just by learning how to get your personal care items for next to free, you'll probably cut your grocery bill in half—or more if you have teenagers!

Target and Walgreens are my two favorite stores to shop because of their amazing store coupons that can then be combined with manufacturers' coupons. This is also the best method for getting your items for next to nothing.

The items I get nearly free from using this method are shampoo, shaving cream, shavers (yes, the nice $10.00 kind), toothpaste, soap, hair spray, deodorant, and so forth. In fact, I do not think I have paid more than $.50 for any of those items in the last four years!

Just by learning how to get your personal care items for next to free, you'll probably cut your grocery bill in half—or more if you have teenagers!

I often hear the argument, "Why use coupons when you can get the generic so much cheaper?"

Insider's Tip: When you combine a coupon with a sale—and even more so when you combine a coupon with a store coupon—you're likely to get your items *much cheaper* than generic. In fact, you could end up with *free products!* You can't get any cheaper than that!

Now you may be asking, "If my item is free, aren't we stealing?" No. Absolutely not! The manufacturer reimburses the store for the value of the coupon plus postage. You're just being a savvy shopper!

The methods I teach and use are store policies and programs that already exist; it's just a matter of your knowing about them. By learning these tricks, you save money—it's as simple as that.

And, as I said before, the store is reimbursed for the manufacturer's coupon, and as for the store coupon, that is a savings policy the store put into place to *lure* you into buying other stuff. But you don't have to fall for it; you can stick to your lists.

Remember, there's marketing at work here: When you purchase the product and use a coupon, the manufacturer is building brand loyalty with you as a consumer and creating a demand for their products; the store is moving products off their shelves plus getting the redemption from the coupon; and you are walking away with a good deal.

It is a win-win situation!

Insider's Tip: When you combine a coupon with a sale—and even more so when you combine a coupon with a store coupon—you're likely to get your items much cheaper than generic. In fact, you could end up with free products! You can't get any cheaper than that!

#7—Change Brands

We all buy different things. My shopping list is not the same as your shopping list. Therefore, I stress strongly that if you do not want to change a single item you buy, that's okay—just find coupons and deals for the products you actually do buy. It is best

I only change brands if a better deal comes along.

for your pocketbook *not* to be brand loyal, but I admit, even I have a few brands that I love!

I only change brands if a better deal comes along.

Let's say you just love Brand X deodorant, and you have been using it for the last ten years. You are aware that it has lost its effectiveness, and you probably are letting off some kind of strange odor, but you just keep buying it because it is what you're used to. But, Brand X typically runs $2.99—even after a coupon.

However, Brand Y is new, and the manufacturer is pushing hard to get Brand Y into your home. Brand Y offers a $2.00 off coupon, which is a rare, high-value coupon that can only lead to a good deal. A week later, you spot Brand Y on sale for only $2.24. What do you do?

My advice: For a risk of only $.24, I would buy Brand Y and try it out. It is a savings of $2.75 in comparison to your old deodorant, and if you do not like it, you have only lost $.24. But, if you do like it, you can buy *twelve* of Brand Y for the price of your one old, nasty deodorant!

This is a deal I just did a few weeks ago, and I am now stocked up on deodorant for the year!

Overall, as I mentioned previously, buying name brand is better with a sale and a coupon and can typically become cheaper than the generic product. However, it is not *wrong* to buy generic.

Insider's Tip: Whole Foods Market offers a wonderful generic brand that holds true to the quality standards they require from all of the products in their store. So, quality-wise, it's great; plus, they offer coupons frequently for their own store brand. So sometimes generic *can* be better.

This might seem like heresy from the 918 Coupon Queen, but keep in mind—gasp!—you will not always have a coupon for *everything* you purchase. Sometimes generic is just going to have to do. But if you want to save mega-money at the grocery store, use my techniques and shop smart!

#8—Different Stores

Each store offers some kind of savings policy—whether they know it or not. It is important that you research the stores around you. You may discover grocery stores that you never knew existed in your city! I found several hidden treasures after I did a little research.

> *Insider's Tip: Whole Foods Market offers a wonderful generic brand that holds true to the quality standards they require from all of the products in their store. So, quality-wise, it's great; plus, they offer coupons frequently for their own store brand. So sometimes generic can be better.*

It may seem odd, but sometimes it's the most expensive stores in your neighborhood that offer the best savings methods.

Find out if the store has a weekly sales ad and when it comes out. Ask if the ad is available online so you can access it early. Then, ask about their savings policies, and find out what they have to offer their customers.

After a quick phone call to one of our local stores, I found out they offered $50.00 coupon books as a fund-raiser. I could call a church/organization participating in the fund-raiser, and I would receive a $50.00 coupon book for only $5.00! A simple phone call can open a door full of savings that you never knew about!

Here's a breakdown of the most common store savings policies:

Price matching:

As discussed earlier, this is a policy where the store will match their competitors' prices. All you have to do is find out which ads they accept, and when you see a good deal, take in your ad and get the price match.

Most of the time when going through the register, there is no need to make a scene and shout to the world, "Hey, I've got coupons here!" Typically you can go through rather quietly and hand the clerk your coupons. However, with price matching it could go a little differently.

Insider's Tip: Hold back the items you are going to price match until the end of the order, and then inform the cashier that you plan on price matching from this point on. If you let the items go through and then you price match, the cashier will have to take all the items out of the bag and search for the prices on the receipt. That would take some time.

You can still use your coupons by simply handing them to the cashier, but the whole process

Insider's Tip: Hold back the items you are going to price match until the end of the order, and then inform the cashier that you plan on price matching from this point on. If you let the items go through and then you price match, the cashier will have to take all the items out of the bag and search for the prices on the receipt. That would take some time.

moves quicker if you let them know you are going to price match. Saving time does everyone a favor!

Frequent Shopper Cards:

Many stores offer sales that can only be had with the use of the stores' Frequent Shopper Card. These are typically free and many times can be linked to online companies such as Upromise.com, which I mentioned earlier, that offer electronic coupons.

Most stores that require such cards will typically feature them in their ads, on their websites, or you'll see them somewhere in the store itself. All you have to do is visit customer service to fill out a form for your free card; then use it every time you shop.

It is not a credit card—it's simply a free shopper's discount card. They use these cards to help ensure repeat customers and possibly to gather demographic information. Make sure you put your coupon e-mail address on the form, since they're sure to send you offers via e-mail!

Some stores also offer Frequent Shopper Cards in the form of punch cards (many coffee shops and specialty stores offer these as well). A local health foods store here has vitamin, bread, and coffee punch cards. If you purchase five packages of bread, you get the sixth one free!

These are great, too, because you can also combine them with coupons for an even better deal.

> *Insider's Tip: Wait until the item goes on sale, use your coupons (if there are ten items in a case, use ten coupons) and then get the 10 percent off!*

Case Discounts:

This one is commonly found in health food stores as well. If you buy a case of a product, you may get a percentage off such as 10 percent. This is not bad—and it's great if you time it right.

Insider's Tip: Wait until the item goes on sale, use your coupons (if there are ten items in a case, use ten coupons) and then get the 10 percent off! (Of course, that is assuming the store you are at will let you use all the savings methods at one time.)

Case discounts can really be useful, especially if you like to stock up or buy in bulk.

Double/Triple Coupons:

I have been teaching workshops for some time, and it still amazes me that people do not know which stores double coupons in our city. Most do not even realize we *have* stores that double coupons.

This is a very important policy that will save you *tons* of money. You not only need to find out if you have stores near you that double or triple coupons, but you also need to find out their limit and policies.

For example,

> **Store #1:** Will double coupons up to and including $.50
> Quaker Granola Bars are on sale for $2.00 per box
> - $.50 manufacturer's coupon
> - $.50 (doubled coupon)
> = $1.00 per box
>
> **Store #2:** Will double up to and including $.25
> Quaker Granola Bars are on sale for $2.00 per box
> - $.50 manufacturer's coupon (it will not double because it has exceeded the store's limit)
> = $1.50 per box

Your best place to shop for Quaker Granola Bars would be store #1.

When you call your store, make sure to ask what days they double (some only double one day out of the month while others double every day). Also, ask if there are any limits. Some stores will let you use as many coupons as you want, while others may limit you to only five coupons doubled per day.

Most stores do not triple every day—in fact, where I live, I have never seen a triple coupon promotion. Usually these happen once a month, quarter, or year. Simply ask customer service.

#9—Know the Lingo

BOGO: Buy One, Get One Free and B1G1: Same as the BOGO coupon

BOGO coupons can be really great coupons when used correctly. There are some stores that will allow you to combine a BOGO coupon with a store BOGO sale. This means both items will be *free!*

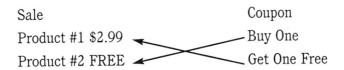

Sale   Coupon

Product #1 $2.99   Buy One

Product #2 FREE   Get One Free

It is almost as if both the coupon and the sale cancel one another out. If your store is running a Buy One, Get One Free promotion, make sure to find out if each item is actually half price or if you literally have to buy one to get one free.

This matters because if the items are actually half price, then you only have to buy one if you only have one coupon or if you only need one.

> *Remember, if you are leaving the store with two products, then you can use two coupons.*

Remember, if you are leaving the store with two products, then you can use two coupons—as long as the coupons are for one product (not $1.00 off the purchase of two of them). Some stores do not allow this, so be sure to ask around first.

10 for $10.00

These are typical marketing techniques to make you think you have to purchase ten of something for it to be only $10.00. If your store requires that, it will mention it on the sales tag in front of the item. (For example, it may say something like, "10 for $10.00 or 1 at $1.39 each). To be a smart shopper, you have to watch the advertising carefully. If your store has a 10 for $10.00 deal, meaning it is only $1.00 each, and you only have five coupons, then you only need to buy five of that product. Some may have limits on how many items you can buy, so be sure to read carefully.

Store Discounts

Many times in store circulars you will see automatic store discounts such as "Buy three and get $3.00 off!" Just know you can use three coupons with those items as long as the coupons are for "$X off one product."

#10—Read the Fine Print

Taking the time to read the coupon itself can work to your advantage. First, it keeps you from making mistakes by purchasing the wrong products. Second, you can find out if the coupon specifies or does not specify a size.

Which means, if your coupon says, "$1.00 off any All Detergent," then you can use that coupon on any size.

Insider's Tip: Sometimes it is better to purchase several of the *smaller* sizes at a cheaper price by using your coupons than it is to purchase the full-size container.

For example:

All Detergent 30 Loads $4.99

- $1/1 manufacturer's coupon

= $3.99 for one All Detergent 30 Loads

OR

All Detergent 2 Loads Travel Size $.99

- $1/1 manufacturer's coupon

= FREE All Detergent 2 loads

> *Insider's Tip: Sometimes it is better to purchase several of the smaller sizes at a cheaper price by using your coupons than it is to purchase the full-size container.*

Since you have followed my strategies and now know how to get several coupons, you'll actually have fifteen All Detergent coupons, right? So here is what the example looks like now:

All Detergent 30 Loads $4.99

- $1/1 manufacturer's coupon

= $3.99 for one All Detergent 30 Loads

OR

15 All Detergent 2 Loads Travel Size at $.99 each

- (15) $1/1 manufacturer's coupons

= 15 All Detergent Travel Size 2 Loads for *FREE*

You now have the thirty loads of All Laundry Detergent completely FREE because you were able to purchase the travel size! Take the travel sizes you purchased and simply pour them into a large container if you want (possibly your old laundry detergent container), and now you have *free* detergent! Now *that's* a 918 Coupon Queen deal!

This isn't just a method for travel sizes; it can work simply on smaller sized products where good sales and good coupons can equal more savings. Remember, by combining sales and good coupons, smaller sized products can actually be a much better deal than the larger ones! And, since you've wisely found multiple coupons, you can actually stock up enough of the smaller size to equal the larger size that you had planned on purchasing.

> *Remember, by combining sales and good coupons, smaller sized products can actually be a much better deal than the larger ones!*

Always read the fine print. Keep in mind that you do have to honor whatever the coupon actually says. If your coupon says, "$1.00 off Colgate Toothpaste 8oz," then that is what you have to purchase. Otherwise it is coupon fraud!

One of the rules on www.918couponqueen.com is that we do not discuss how to misuse coupons because coupon fraud is illegal, and the misuse of coupons costs stores money and forces them to change their policies—costing us *all* money! Plus, when using the coupons in their correct form, you can still have a multitude of savings!

#11—Use Multiple Transactions

It is possible that your store may limit the number of coupons you may use, rewards you may redeem, and so forth. If that is the case, don't despair: Simply use multiple transactions!

For example, if your store's policy states that they will only double one like coupon per transaction but you have three of those coupons, split your transaction into three separate transactions. Most stores do allow this without a problem. All you have to do is ask if they are okay with it, then use the divider to split your transaction. Now you will be able to use all your coupons!

If your store will not allow separate transactions, you can always come back at another time. I have known many couponers who simply walk out the door, put their stuff in the car, and head back into the store. Again, we have to honor what the policy states and what the store will allow. But, many times, using multiple transactions is a simple way to get a good deal with one trip!

#12—Unadvertised Sales

The average grocery circular is not that big and therefore does not allow the store to put all their sales items into the flyer. Also, many stores allow managers to decide some sales.

I have been teaching Buying Organic on a Budget workshops at our local Whole Foods. Whole Foods has a weekly sales flyer, and it's pretty small. However, when you step in the actual store, you'll find *tons* of sales items.

Remember, the best deals are where you find them—even when a store appears to be more expensive!

This is another reason why you need to get to know the stores around you. Even if you have never walked into them before, now is a good time to check them out. Sometimes the best deals can be found in stores that seem more expensive.

Many times you can find unadvertised sales listed on our 918 Coupon Queen forums, and if you find a sale, be sure to post it so everyone can grab the deal!

#13—Saving Money on Meat

The following information is from the USDA Food Safety and Inspection Service website:

Types of Dates

- A "**Sell-By**" date tells the store how long to display the product for sale. You should buy the product before the date expires.

- A "**Best if Used By (or Before)**" date is recommended for best flavor or quality. It is not a purchase or safety date.

- A "**Use-By**" date is the last date recommended for the use of the product while at peak quality. The manufacturer of the product has determined the date.

At Walmart and Sam's, they will actually begin to clearance out their meat a few days before the sell-by date. This means you can actually find clearance meat, and all you have to do is take it home and freeze it. Typically, the sell-by dates are every thirty days, so by using this method, you can stock up for one month and then go back for more. You can also ask employees in the meat department when the markdowns will begin.

Target is another store that will mark down meat. They use peelies on their meat products as well. I bought chicken the other day that was on sale for $2.99 per pound, plus there was a peelie store coupon on the package for $2.50 off! One pound of chicken only cost me $.49!

Again, what is important is that you find out what the stores near you offer. Some will have twelve-hour meat sales, and even specialty meat stores offer great deals. All it takes to find them is a phone call.

We have a national meat factory that offers once-a-month dock sales. It's restaurant-quality meat at rock bottom prices. I once paid $113 for two months' worth of meat for my whole family!

Many times it is the unusual places that we would not normally expect that offer the best deals. Ask around and find out what is going on in your town.

Now that you know some of the basics of good couponing, let's move on to some more advanced couponing techniques!

Advanced Couponing Techniques

"The LORD your God is with you, he is mighty to save. He will take great delight in you, he will quiet you with his love, he will rejoice over you with singing" (Zephaniah 3:17).

Chapter Summary:

- Rain Checks
- Item Substitution
- Overage
- Rebates

Have you mastered the 13 Ways to Save, and would you like to save even more? Well, buckle your seat belts; we're moving into Advanced Coupon Techniques!

#1—Rain Checks

Here's something to keep you dry on a rainy day—rain checks. Put simply, rain checks are given if the item you are at the store for is out of stock. So if you are psyched about a great sale and you walk in the door only to find that another couponer beat you to the deal, never fear—ask for a rain check!

You can use your coupons with the rain check!

Many times rain checks do not expire, and they hold the sale until that item comes back in stock. Even more importantly, you can use your coupons with the rain check! Rain checks are not coupons; they are actual sales. They allow you to "capture the sale" and use it at a later date.

Want to make this even better? As an avid couponer, I know certain coupons come out on a regular basis, and I also know the sales cycles. If it is a BBQ item, for example, I know there is likely to be a coupon out for that item in the summer. Therefore, if the sale is great, I can grab a rain check and hold onto it until I get my coupons for that item.

Maybe it's an item that you can buy coupons for on eBay. If that's the case, wait until the end of the sales week, when the product is likely to be out of stock. Ask for your rain check, and then hold onto it until your coupons come in the mail. Then, take your rain check and your coupons back to the store! You didn't miss a deal at all; in fact, maybe you even got a *better deal* by waiting for the coupons!

Maybe you already have a well-stocked stockpile but you know the sale is a good one. Grab a rain check and use it when your stock diminishes! Or, maybe you have a well-packed freezer with not an inch of room left. That's okay—grab a rain check, and when your freezer space frees up, go grab the deal!

Here's what to ask your store about rain checks:

- Does your store offer rain checks?
- Do the rain checks expire?
- Can you use the rain check to purchase more than one product?
- Does the store substitute an item instead of issuing a rain check?

Make a separate tab in your coupon organizer for rain checks. Store them where they are easy to find, and you'll be able to grab one whenever you see a coupon to combine with it. Remember, you don't have to use a rain check; if you decide that deal wasn't so great after all, don't worry about it.

> *Remember, you don't have to use a rain check; if you decide that deal wasn't so great after all, don't worry about it.*

Insider's Tip: Many times you can get a rain check for a specific flavor, too! If you want ham and cheese Hot Pockets and all that's left on the shelf is pepperoni, then ask for a rain check!

#2—Item Substitution

There are a few stores that do not issue rain checks; instead they do what is called "item substitution." For example, let's say you go into your favorite grocery store to grab a store brand cereal that is on sale for only $1.49, but when you get to the aisle, you find your cereal all gone.

Insider's Tip: Many times you can get a rain check for a specific flavor, too!

You ask a nearby employee for a rain check, but instead he offers you the name brand cereal...for the same price! That's called item substitution and can often lead to an even *better* deal, especially if you have a coupon for the item you picked out.

This is a concept that can work anywhere, not just at the grocery store. Many stores want you to purchase your items that day while you are in the store. With a rain check, you are more likely to not complete your purchase. So they'll offer you another item and make the sale.

#3—Overage: Making Money at the Store

This is a concept that is always a favorite in my workshops. How can we *make* money at the grocery store?

When I did my first TV interview, I got to the station extra early just to be prepared. I ended up sitting in the waiting room for quite some time chatting about coupons with the secretary. She told me a story about her grandmother. Her grandmother used coupons regularly and one day decided she was going to show the rest of the family how to do it. They all went to the store and watched as the cashier subtracted coupon after coupon and the deals rang up. In the end, the cashier gave the woman *$60.00* for shopping at that particular grocery store! Literally, she walked out with $60.00 in cash!

You're probably thinking, "How awesome it would be if stores still did this!" I am sure many of us would take up couponing quickly! We have to get a little more creative nowadays with something called Overage (or Moneymaker), but you can still create some *amazing* deals!

Here's how it works:

Shampoo $2.00 per bottle

- $2.50 manufacturer's coupon

= +$.50

In the end, the cashier gave the woman $60.00 for shopping at that particular grocery store!

The store is not going to hand you back $.50 for buying that shampoo. So what happens? If the one bottle of shampoo is all you buy, the register will automatically break even and you'll owe nothing but sales tax. However, when the store turns in that coupon for redemption, they'll be getting $2.00 back even though you did not actually use all of that $2.00.

If you added a $.50 package of gum to that transaction, the coupon would automatically remove $2.00, which would make your gum *completely free!* The $2.00 off would attach itself to the entire transaction!

This is where having multiple coupons comes in handy. If you bought twenty of those shampoos for $2.00 and used twenty coupons, you'd have $10.00 in overage! That means you could purchase anything in the store, and that $10.00 would be deducted from the total!

Some stores allow overage on a regular basis while others will adjust the coupon manually so that it does not allow for overage. After shopping at your favorite stores for a while, you will learn which ones allow this and which ones don't.

Just this week I bought five items at $1.00 each and gave the cashier five coupons for $2.00 off. He manually adjusted the

This is where having multiple coupons comes in handy. If you bought twenty of those shampoos for $2.00 and used twenty coupons, you'd have $10.00 in overage!

coupons and would not allow the overage. The funny thing is, when the store turns in the coupon for reimbursement they will get reimbursed the whole $2.00. Bum deal for me, but the store liked those coupons!

The most common Moneymakers are travel size items when the coupon has no size specifics. However, high-value coupons straight from the manufacturer can easily make you money when combined with a good sale.

"Free" is still a great deal, but the *best* deals are *better than free!* Keep an eye on our forums and blog, and when you see Moneymaker, you know to get your coupons ready and be prepared for great deals ahead!

#4—Rebates

I had heard of using rebates to make money years ago, but I could never quite figure out how to do it. It does take a bit more time, but if you are willing, rebates can bring a surprise to your mailbox every week!

Let's look at a few different types of rebates.

A. Cash Back Rebates:

When a company is launching a new product, rebates are a great way to get that product into a consumer's home. After all, how many people never redeem the rebate?

Here are a few examples of Cash Back Rebates:

- Buy $10.00 of Product X and you'll get $5.00 back!
- Buy 15 products from Company X and you'll get $10.00 back!

"Free" is still a great deal, but the best deals are better than free!

The "Buy X number of products" is clever because folks will go purchase the products and never send off for the rebate; or when they do, they may find that they have purchased the wrong products and don't even qualify.

However, when used properly, these types of rebates can be gold mines! Why? You can use your coupons too! Use a coupon when you purchase rebated products to get the final price down as low as possible, and then submit your rebate. You'll still get the check!

B. Free After Rebate/Try Me Free Offers

If a company has launched a fabulous product, the best way to market that product is by making it free! After all, who wouldn't try a bag of buffalo potato chips that literally burn the taste buds off of your tongue? It's free!

Plus, the increase in sales will lead to better shelf position of that product at the store and will also give the company valuable information and sign-ups for future newsletters and coupons. Thus, the company knows its target market and has their contact information, too!

These types of rebates tend to be located on the company website or in the e-newsletters. Occasionally, you will see these offers in a newspaper as well.

These are great for consumers because, again, you can pair up your rebate with a coupon (if one is available), and you'll end up getting a rebate check for the full amount of that product!

Use a coupon when you purchase rebated products to get the final price down as low as possible, and then submit your rebate. You'll still get the check!

Here's an example:

Excedrin PM $3.99
- $2.00 store coupon
- $1.00 manufacturer's coupon
= $.99 out of pocket!

But, the manufacturer has a rebate available for the retail price of that product, which is $3.99. If I submit my receipt and my rebate, I'll get a check for $3.99—the retail price of the product— even though I paid only $.99! I just made $3.00 by purchasing Excedrin! Great deal!

In some cases, the manufacturers will adjust the rebate much like the overage concept, but most times it works perfectly.

C. Satisfaction Guaranteed/Money Back Guarantee

These types of rebates are commonly found on the packages themselves. These are the "If you aren't satisfied with our product, you'll get your money back" type of rebates. I do not recommend you do these if you really are satisfied. But if you have questions about whether or not you apply for the rebate, contact the company and ask directly.

I have seen other coupon sites promote these types of rebates. However, if I truly like the product, it seems dishonest to submit a rebate telling the company that I did not like it.

Essentially, you can make money by doing rebates. However, I think many companies have caught onto that idea and a new trend has arisen. Lately, I have seen many rebates in the form of actual coupons. For example, one may say,

"Purchase $10.00 in Brand X and you'll get $20.00 in coupons" rather than cash.

This is still a good deal, but it takes some of the fun out of watching for checks in your mailbox.

Now that you know some of the great things about rebates, let's look at the mechanics so you can be sure to get your rebates back.

Tips for submitting rebates

1. Read the form very carefully. If you make even *one* mistake, your rebate could be void. Even something as simple as putting it in the wrong envelope could cost you your rebate.

2. Submit the original receipt. If you have several items you are purchasing for different rebates, then it is best to do multiple transactions. You'll split up your order and end up with multiple receipts to submit.

3. Make sure the rebate is available in your area. Some rebates are only for certain areas of the country, so be sure to read carefully.

4. Wait it out. It can take as long as twelve weeks to receive your rebate. There are ways to track them online. Simply search for "rebate tracking," and you'll find a few clearinghouses that will help you

Remember: Write down on a 3x5 card the information for the rebate including a company contact number and the date you submitted it so you can keep track of your rebates.

track your rebate. Sometimes even the companies themselves offer tracking services.

Remember: Write down on a 3x5 card the information for the rebate including a company contact number and the date you submitted it so you can keep track of your rebates. Store that card in a file or some kind of box and periodically go through it to call companies that have not sent you back your rebate. This can really help you keep track of your money and make sure you get back all that you sent in for. Also, be patient and realize that sometimes they just don't come back. If you do a lot of rebates, you'll soon realize that some just never make it back. I do not know why that is—maybe sneaky marketing or maybe it just got lost in the multitudes. Keeping the company information on file can help you contact them if there is an issue, but every once in a while you just have to let one go.

CHAPTER 8

The Drugstore Secrets

"The secret things belong to the LORD our God, but the things revealed belong to us and to our children forever, that we may follow all the words of this law" (Deuteronomy 29:29).

Chapter Highlights:

- CVS Pharmacy
- Walgreens

For years I completely avoided drugstores. One quick walk through can tell you how expensive they actually are. It struck me as odd when I found out that drugstores can be the best source of savings. In fact, our local drugstores account for probably 75 percent of all the free stuff I have gotten in the last few years!

Although I use the word "secrets" for the title of this chapter, these saving methods are no secret. Remember, I am simply teaching you techniques that already exist—you just have to

Drugstores can be the best source of savings. Our local drugstores account for probably 75 percent of all the free stuff I have gotten in the last few years!

learn about them and know how to use them to your advantage!

I wanted to give you a quick overview of the two most popular drugstores for couponers. There are many others scattered throughout the country, so be sure to find out their policies, as these hidden treasures will turn out to be a valuable blessing to your family!

The policies below are up to date at the time of the writing of this book. Please verify the policy before shopping at your local store by contacting the following drugstores directly.

CVS Pharmacy

Once you master the art of CVS, you'll be in love for years to come. First, you have to get a CVS Extra Care Card, which we've talked about before. You can do this by signing up for free online at CVS.com or in the actual store.

Extra Care Bucks: ECBs are like cash and are printed onto your receipt when you purchase qualifying products. Check your weekly ad to find out what products qualify. For example, one might read, "Purchase $20.00 in Cover Girl makeup and you'll receive $5.00 in Extra Care Bucks."

But you must be sure to save the receipt!

Remember, the required amount you must purchase is calculated *before* coupons. This means you can use your coupons to get that total down but still be earning ECBs because it is calculated by the actual price of the product.

Also, you do not have to purchase the total required amount in one transaction, since it is tied to your CVS card. You can actually purchase the required products *at any CVS store at any time*—as long as it is during the time period that the promotion is being offered.

Remember, the required amount you must purchase is calculated before coupons.

You'll want to visit www.918couponqueen.com to find great deal scenarios before you hit the store. The best ECB offers are ones that are already free after ECBs; you'll find those highlighted in the weekly ad.

The best way to use ECBs to your advantage is to make sure your OOP (out-of-pocket expense) is low and that you are actually earning a profit from the ECBs. To do this, you can "stack" your manufacturers' coupons plus the store coupons. You can also use money-off coupons such as $5.00 off $25.00 that CVS occasionally distributes.

For example,

> Garnier Hair spray is $2.00 plus if you buy two, you'll get $2.00 in ECBs
>
> (2) Garnier Hair sprays = $4.00
>
> - $1/1 manufacturer's coupon
>
> - $1/1 manufacturer's coupon
>
> - $1/2 CVS store coupon
>
> = $1.00 for 2 Garnier Hair sprays out of pocket

Plus, you earned $2.00 in ECBs, so you just made $1.00 for buying something you need!

Remember, ECBs will expire four weeks from the day they were printed.

> *Remember, ECBs will expire four weeks from the day they were printed.*

Wow, now you know how to make money from using ECBs—but that's not all! You can also learn how to "roll" your ECBs. Essentially, rolling ECBs means to use the ECBs from your last purchase to minimize your out-of-pocket expense on your next purchase and to be sure you are purchasing items that will generate more ECBs.

For example,

Purchase three Cover Girl Items ($3.99 each) and get $10.00 in ECBs

(3) Cover Girl Items = $11.97 total

- (3) $2/1 Manufacturer's Coupons

= (3) Cover Girl items for only **$5.97**

And, you earned $10.00 in ECBs!

Next transaction, let's say this happens:

Purchase three Cover Girl items for $11.97 total

- (3) $2/1 coupons

- $10.00 ECBs

(You'll have to add $4 in items as fillers to make the most of your $10.00 ECB)

= **FREE** Cover Girl items, *and* you generated another $10.00 ECBs!

If the offer is unlimited, then you can do this as often as you like during the promotional period, earning more ECBs and earning more free products. If it is unlimited and you do several of these promotions in one transaction, you will earn one large

ECB total, but you'll be out more out of pocket since you won't be "rolling" your ECBs.

Insider's Tip: Keep a close eye out, though, as some ECB promotions can limit you to only one per week or month. So sign up other family members for CVS loyalty cards to keep you getting the great deals!

Dollar off coupons are another way to save at CVS. These are coupons for a certain dollar amount off when another amount is spent. These are randomly generated on your receipt and also come via snail mail. Watch the 918 Coupon Queen Forums for those!

> *Insider's Tip: Keep a close eye out, though, as some ECB promotions can limit you to only one per week or month. So sign up other family members for CVS loyalty cards to keep you getting the great deals!*

When you check out at the register, be sure to give the cashier your CVS dollar-off coupons first. (If you have a "$5.00 off a $50.00 purchase" coupon and you get your total down to only $10.00 after all your other coupons, then the $5.00 off $50.00 will *not* work.) Next, give the cashier your store coupons, and then give her your manufacturer's coupons.

CRTs are also a great savings program offered by CVS. CRT stands for Cash Register Tape, and basically, they are coupons generated by your purchase (somewhat randomly) and can be used only by you since you are the CVS cardholder. CRTs are CVS store coupons, and your purchases will trigger these coupons to print.

Rain Checks: CVS also offers rain checks if your item is out of stock and even if it is for an item that generates ECBs! It never hurts to ask for a rain check!

When you check out at the register, be sure to give the cashier your CVS dollar-off coupons first.

CVS is a gold mine for great deals. By using their ECBs and CRTs and plain old manufacturers' coupons, you may end up with tons of *free* or *nearly free* products!

I realize all these abbreviations and new methods of shopping can be a bit confusing. Please ask your questions in our 918 Coupon Queen Forums at http://www.918couponqueen.com!

Walgreens

Walgreens is also a great drugstore to add to your coupon round-up. Like CVS, Walgreens has also rolled out many ways to save.

Register Rewards: RRs print out at the end of your transaction when you purchase qualifying products. You will find those products listed in the weekly ad. An example might be, "Purchase X and get $2.00 in Register Rewards."

Remember, you can use your coupons to get the initial price of that product down and then purchase the item and generate your Register Reward.

You cannot purchase several of those items at one time and get multiple Register Rewards if it is the same deal. You can purchase two totally separate deals at the same time even if they both generate Register Rewards. The RRs will print out for both deals.

This basically means if Ragu is on sale "Buy two, get $1.00 in RRs," you can't buy six at one time in one transaction to get $3.00 in RRs. You'll have to come back into the store later or go to another store to purchase more products for those particular Register Rewards.

Walgreens RRs can be used like cash on products throughout the store. RRs do act just like manufacturers' coupons, though, so if you have an RR to redeem and you have manufacturers' coupons to use with it, then you will need to use a few fillers.

This means if you are purchasing one box of cereal for $3.00 with $3.00 in RRs and you also have a $1/1 manufacturer's coupon, then you'll need to get something small—a "filler" for that second coupon to attach itself to in the computer. It can be something like a $.25 pencil or a pack of gum; it doesn't matter.

Remember, you can use your coupons to get the initial price of that product down and then purchase the item and generate your Register Reward.

You cannot combine two manufacturers' coupons on one product, and an RR is a manufacturer's coupon.

Insider's Tip: The nice thing is that Walgreens typically offers several items that are *free* after RRs, and when you use your coupons with those items, you have yourself a moneymaker! This is a great way to get some extra groceries free!

Walgreens also offers store coupons. Store coupons can be found in the weekly ad, promotional advertising throughout the store such as kids' activity books, health savings books, and so forth. Store coupons can be combined with manufacturers' coupons for an even better deal!

Walgreens offers money-off coupons frequently on their website, such as coupons for $5.00 off the purchase of $25.00. These coupons typically state that your total has to be $25.00 or more *after* coupons. To make the most of this deal, you would want to purchase items that generate RRs.

Insider's Tip: The nice thing is that Walgreens typically offers several items that are free after RRs, and when you use your coupons with those items, you have yourself a money-maker! This is a great way to get some extra groceries free!

In a sense, saving money at drugstores becomes a game. It can be a bit tricky, but in the long run it really pays off. Walgreens was the first store I began to use for couponing at drugstores; it is the number-one place where I have scored all my free toothpaste, deodorant, shampoo, razors, and soap! Just by cutting those personal item expenses, we cut our grocery bill by *hundreds of dollars* a year! Just think how fast those $5.00 shampoos and $10.00 razors add up!

The only way you'll get good at couponing is by practice. It may take a bit of time, but after awhile you'll be running around, gathering up items for next to nothing for your family—and to bless other families as well.

In the meantime, if you do have questions, ask away on www.918couponqueen.com. We're all in this thing together! Don't get discouraged; if you mess up what you thought was going to be a good deal, don't worry. Another good deal is on its way!

So now that you have the scoop on the drugstores, which can seem the most expensive of all, let's get down to some specialty requirements. My son Elisha has to eat very carefully, so by necessity I learned about how to buy organic without breaking the bank.

Read on and I'll show you how, too!

Buying Organic without Breaking the Bank

"Observe the commands of the LORD your God, walking in his ways and revering him. For the LORD your God is bringing you into a good land—a land with streams and pools of water, with springs flowing in the valleys and hills; a land with wheat and barley, vines and fig trees, pomegranates, olive oil and honey; a land where bread will not be scarce and you will lack nothing; a land where the rocks are iron and you can dig copper out of the hills. When you have eaten and are satisfied, praise the LORD your God for the good land he has given you" (Deuteronomy 8:6-10).

Chapter Highlights

- Going Organic and Saving Money
- Where to Start

- Finding Organic Coupons
- Go Green—At Home!
- Bulk Discounts

> *I am all about buying organic and eating healthy, and God designed us to eat healthy.*

I am all about buying organic and eating healthy, and I would say, judging by the scripture from Deuteronomy 8, that God designed us to eat healthy. God not only wants you to be able to eat, but He also wants you to eat well.

There is a very common myth that couponing is only for processed, boxed foods, but that is not the case. Although it does take a little more digging, finding coupons for organic products can be done using the methods in Chapter Four.

Here are a few of my favorite ways to find coupons for organic products:

1. I was once a taste tester for a company that produces organic products. Always, always call the manufacturer. Let them know how often you buy their products and how much you love them, and then ask for coupons. You can then ask if you can call back for more at a later date.

   I was once a taste taster for an organic company. I simply called the company and told them how much I loved them. They not only sent me coupons but also sent us a case of their product to try so I could give my opinions! Calling goes a long way!

2. Visit Mambosprouts.com for printable organic coupons and also the opportunity to sign up for their amazing

coupon book. They distribute it a few times a year, and it is packed full of coupons for popular organic products.

Mambo Sprouts also produces the store coupons found in *The Whole Deal Newsletter* at the front of Whole Foods Market stores.

3. Visit your favorite natural foods store for extra discounts. Whole Foods, for example, offers *The Whole Deal Newsletter,* which is packed full of store coupons for great products—even on their store brand!

Going organic and saving money

As I mentioned earlier, I have been teaching Buying Organic on a Budget workshops at our local Whole Foods Market for some time, and I was very surprised to learn about all the savings methods Whole Foods offers.

Avoiding a specialty store may be costing you some savings!

Remember, the most expensive stores do tend to be the ones with the best coupon policies. Be sure to call your local health store and ask the same questions you would at a traditional grocery store. Avoiding a specialty store may be costing you some savings!

Don't forget, in *most* stores, you can combine a store coupon with a manufacturer's coupon for an even better deal—even in health food stores!

If you are switching to organic completely, be sure to learn how to cook from scratch in order to save money. Follow the sales ads and buy what you have coupons for; learn how to cook around that. When you purchase an already boxed item, you are likely paying for convenience more than anything else.

We saved nearly $40.00 a month by buying a popcorn popper and popping our own popcorn! My son Elisha loves popcorn, and it is very expensive to buy allergy-free popcorn for the microwave. So, we invested $14.00 in a popcorn popper and literally saved hundreds of dollars!

Many of the same principles listed in the previous chapters will apply to organic shopping as well. Even though the prices for organic products do run a bit higher, it is money invested into the health of you and your family—in my opinion, something well worth it!

Insider's Tip: See if your favorite store offers bulk bins. These are great ways to stock up on cereals, rice, beans, legumes, and granola. They are convenient; plus, if your recipe only calls for one cup of flour, then that is all you have to buy. You skip the boxed convenience, lowering your price a bit, and you can measure out exactly what you need!

Where to start

Most of us have only begun to buy organic and are merely taking baby steps. There are a few foods that you should start with if you would like to start purchasing organic. A few foods that tend to be highest in pesticides, hormones, and/or antibiotics include the following:

- Bananas
- Kiwi
- Mangoes
- Papaya
- Pineapples
- Oranges
- Celery
- Potatoes
- Spinach
- Bell Peppers
- Lettuce
- Tomatoes
- Green Beans
- Beef
- Dairy
- Pork
- Poultry
- Eggs

Data taken from Smartmoney.com. (They got the data from "Eating Between the Lines," Environmental Working Group and Consumer Reports.)

Finding organic coupons

Did you know many companies that produce organic dairy products also offer coupons? Visit sites such as Horizonorganic.com and

Organicvalley.com. Coupons for organic products are available; you just have to look for them.

Here are a few companies that offer coupons for their organic products on a regular basis:

- Mambosprouts.com
- Deliciouslivingmag.com/coupons/
- Earthsbest.com
- Morningstarfarms.com
- Kashi.com
- Browncowfarm.com
- Stoneyfieldfarms.com
- Enjoylifefoods.com

There are many, many more available. Simply visit the site of your favorite brand!

Finding good produce

One of the most common questions I receive in reference to eating healthy is, "How can I find a good deal on produce?"

That is a very good question, and I will tell you it is unlikely that you will find coupons for broccoli or grapes—not unheard of, just not that common. The best way to save money on fruits and vegetables is simply to purchase them in season and then learn how to freeze/can them for year-round use. It is a simple process that can be easily learned online.

Also, buying frozen fruits and vegetables during the winter months can bring relief to your wallet. If you are daring, cook around what produce is in season. Break out of the few fruits you or your children are willing to eat and try something new!

Insider's Tip: Check out local farmers markets. This is a great way to shop locally, buy healthy, and save money. Many farms will actually let you come out and pick the fruit and vegetables yourself. These can be great family outings and also a way to teach your children about eating healthy!

Browse the Internet for a while and search for local farmers markets, and visit Pickyourown.org to find a local farm near you.

Go green—at home!

It does not take much to grow your own garden, either, and this can be the best money-saver of all.

Make it a family project: Have your children pick the spot and help sow the seed so your family can reap a good organic harvest. It is a great feeling to know exactly what your family is putting into their bodies! Growing just a few of your favorite fruits and veggies can ease the strain on your pocketbook when you are trying to eat healthy.

Insider's Tip: Check out local farmers markets. This is a great way to shop locally, buy healthy, and save money. Many farms will actually let you come out and pick the fruit and vegetables yourself. These can be great family outings and also a way to teach your children about eating healthy!

Bulk discounts

If you do shop at specialty food stores, be sure to ask about a bulk discount. Buying in bulk for traditional items is usually not a good idea because so many bulk stores do not allow coupons. It is actually better to buy the items individually and use coupons than to buy into the convenience of bulk buying.

However, most of the natural foods stores near me offer case discounts. This means it actually does save you money to buy in bulk, especially when those items are on sale already.

Here's an example of how this could work for you:

Organic Cookies regular price: $3.99

Organic Cookies on sale for $2.99

Purchase a case and save 10% (eight boxes of cookies)

If you purchase these cookies all the time, a case may work well for you and help you stock up and save money.

Purchasing eight individual boxes of Organic Cookies would normally cost $31.92.

Purchasing eight individual boxes of Organic Cookies on sale costs $23.92.

Purchasing an eight-box case on sale with the case discount costs $21.59!

Therefore, your best way to save would be to purchase the case when it is on sale. If your store lets you add coupons to that, you can slash your prices even more!

Remember, it's not that you are changing what you buy; you are simply changing how you buy it.

Remember, it's not that you are changing what you buy; you are simply changing how you buy it. Eating healthy is good for your family and does not have to break the bank.

So there you have it—buying organic on a budget. If you stay sharp, keep a watchful eye, and even try your hand at gardening, you can make a switch to eating organic without ruining your bank account.

Now that you have a handle on that, let's get on to another good topic. We've already talked about moneymakers—deals that actually put money back into your pocket. Now let's go a bit further with how to make a little extra money on the side.

Making a Little Extra on the Side

"She watches over the affairs of her household and does not eat the bread of idleness. Her children arise and call her blessed; her husband also, and he praises her" (Proverbs 31:27-28).

Chapter Highlights:

- Couponing
- Teaching a Class
- Starting a Blog
- Mystery Shopping
- Filling Out Online Surveys
- Earning Points
- Getting Money Back
- Selling on Craigslist and eBay

- Having a Garage Sale
- Reviewing Products

The virtuous woman not only watched over her household but she also had a business on the side. When I became a stay-at-home mom, I did everything to make money, but only a few of them actually worked.

Deuteronomy 8:18 says, *"But remember the LORD your God, for it is he who gives you the ability to produce wealth, and so confirms his covenant, which he swore to your forefathers, as it is today."*

God gives you the ability to produce wealth—did you catch that? Notice first that it takes *ability* to get wealth; then notice that it is *God* who gives that ability. That means you don't need to ask your friends what you should be doing; nor do you need to be worried about it all day long. You need to pray to the One who gives you the ability!

Ask God what He would have you do; ask Him to lead you in the right direction and PUT people in your path who will help you discover what you should be doing.

> *Insider's Tip: God will not take you out of everything you know and make you do something totally off the wall that has nothing to do with the natural abilities or gifts that He has put in you.*

Insider's Tip: God will not take you out of everything you know and make you do something totally off the wall that has nothing to do with the natural abilities or gifts that He has put in you. God will nudge you one step at a time. When you complete step one, God will move you on to steps two and three. Most successful Christians did not jump from step one to step six; they took it one step at a time as God moved them.

In saying that, here are a few things I actually did from home to bring in extra money:

Couponing

I know you've read all about it at this point. However, we're talking saving 50 percent on your bill, so think about it like this: Say you spend $600 a month on groceries for your family, and now, by spending some extra time planning and cutting a few coupons, you're saving *$300* a month! That's putting $300 back in your pocket!

You can do a little or you can do a lot, but at least do something! It is time for us to stop spending needlessly and wasting money in the name of convenience. Not only that, these amazing techniques will actually put hundreds of dollars back in your wallet. And it may be just enough to keep you from having to get a second job or even enough to get you out of debt!

This is not one of those things that will take you months to see the results. You will see the results the very first time you shop!

Teaching a Class

If you have a hobby that you think others would benefit from, call your local community centers. My friend who hooked me up with the community center teaches jewelry making. You can teach virtually anything you're good at or at which you have experience, from how to buy a home to public speaking. If you have a talent, don't hide it—teach it to others! You'll help those around you, and you'll earn a little extra money too!

If you do not have access to a community center, see if you can hold classes at a church or restaurant. Don't try to do something you are not called to do, though. If public speaking is not a gift God has given to you, then try something else. Every method is not for every person. God has given each of us unique talents and abilities—use what God has given you.

Starting a blog

Do you have something you are passionate about? Blogging is all the rage these days simply because sites like Blogger.com and Wordpress.com offer blogging websites completely *free*. Log on, follow the steps, and create a site for your business, hobby, or even just for you personally.

Not only can you put ads on these sites through various affiliate marketing firms, but when you develop a sound product, you can also sell your ads privately.

Let's say you are very opinionated about football in your state. Your blog is unique, you've mastered social media sites like Twitter and Facebook, and you have promoted your blog all over the place.

Now you have a solid stream of traffic coming in, and you approach your local college and ask them to advertise. They do, and then you approach your local sporting goods store and ask them to advertise. They do as well! Now you are making a steady income off of the ads you have privately sold on your blog—all for talking about something you love!

It is an amazing opportunity; however, it takes a lot of work to build. You also have to have a blog with good, unique content. After you build it up, you can spend a little money to get a professional blog design and create a slick look and brand. Like I said, it does take work, but if you have unique content and you believe God has given you something to share, then go for it!

Blogging is something I am very well versed in at the moment, since I also operate a blog site. However, I must say if you do decide to go out on a limb and start a coupon blog, remember that there are hundreds of them and you will have to have content that stands out from the crowd. The same thing goes for the mommy bloggers as well. If you want to use your blog to make money from home, really ask God for direction and pray about your content.

Mystery Shopping

A mystery shopper is someone hired by a company to go into a business, let's say a restaurant, order food, ask questions, and then report about the experience. I have done this multiple times at banks, restaurants, stores, and so forth.

I'd get an assignment, go to the restaurant and order food, and then I would make sure to have a special request of some sort. I would pay very careful attention to the response of the employees, the time it took for the food to be made, the time it took to get my check, and the overall experience.

918 Coupon Queen tip: Remember, no company should ever ask for your credit card information.

I'd turn in my report that night, and then I would get a check to cover my meal and a few extra dollars to cover gas. This is not a huge moneymaking opportunity; however, it did allow us to go out to eat every now and again for basically nothing!

There are many reputable mystery-shopping companies out there; a little research online should turn up the good ones. 918 Coupon Queen tip: Remember, no company should ever ask for your credit card information. You are not buying anything from them.

Filling Out Online Surveys

Would you be willing to get paid for taking surveys? Companies like Pinecone Research actually offer free products and/or cash for you to take surveys—really! The surveys will vary for different products and/or companies, but you are rewarded for those that you complete. The trick is to find legitimate survey companies. There are several out there, and again, a simple Google search can find them.

Again, never give out your credit card number for any reason. Some of the sites do require you to have a PayPal account in order to receive your money. Use wisdom and discretion, and if it is a legitimate company, then it may be okay.

I did online surveys for a while on sites that allow you to build up points and then redeem those points for gift cards. Now, I do not have the extra time that it takes to complete some of these surveys. However, at the time, they helped a great deal. I got gift cards to restaurants, grocery stores, and home improvement stores! There was also a time when I would get these gift cards, use them to buy an item, and then give that item as a Christmas or birthday gift because we couldn't spend extra money on anything; I had to get creative about how to buy gifts. I earned those gift cards, believe me; they did take time, but it was well worth it in the end. I was able to buy things that our family needed and normally would not have been able to purchase.

Earning Points

Sites like Mypoints.com or Swagbucks.com allow you to earn points that are then redeemed for gift cards or products. Right now, I am earning a digital camera through Swagbucks.com. How am I doing it? Swagbucks.com, for example, allows you to earn points simply by searching the site. The search engine is powered by Google, so many times I get the same results. I downloaded the toolbar and use it as my main search engine to help rack up points.

I also signed up a few years ago at BzzAgent.com. Through BzzAgent, I can join a campaign to review a product. I get the product, review it, spread the word about the product, and then write up reports. I can then earn points through Mypoints.com by turning in my BzzAgent.com reports! I've earned several gift cards this way.

In my opinion, point sites are a great option because they don't involve cash. No money is exchanged; you simply follow their guidelines and answer surveys, search, shop or whatever, and earn points. It's easy and simple, and you'll reap some great rewards.

Be warned though, these things can be addicting!

Getting Money Back

Ever heard of Ebates.com or Cashbaq.com? These are online rebate sites. Let's say you are going to shop online—you would simply go to one of these sites and shop through them first, because they probably link to the store at which you'd shop anyway. Then you earn a rebate off of the total amount you spend at that store.

If you do a lot of online shopping, this is a great way to get money back in your pocket. I personally do most of my shopping online simply because of the great deals I can find. Signing up for these sites is easy, and you can sign up for different ones too.

Just try it out and see if it works for you. If you own a business, definitely try these sites out. You are already spending the money, so you might as well try a few techniques that may help you spend less.

Don't just limit yourself to saving money at the grocery store—save money everywhere you go!

Companies spend thousands of dollars every year on paper, pens, ink, computers, and so on. By learning how to buy these at the right store and at the right time, they could literally cut their expenses in half without cutting their items or their employees!

Don't just limit yourself to saving money at the grocery store—save money everywhere you go!

Selling on Craigslist and eBay

This was my first method of making extra money. I started selling items on eBay when I was in college. I never really stuck to something particular—well, okay, there was a time that I made tie-dyed curtains and tried to sell a few of those. Ah, the good ol' days.

I actually did best-selling antique and flea market items. I do have just enough knowledge in that area to make me dangerous, and my dad and grandparents have always been big on antiques. My dad would find things for me to sell, and he also helped me learn to find things that would sell well on the Internet.

What I learned quickly, though, is that things that are hard to find here in Oklahoma may not be hard to find somewhere else in the country. Sometimes I would think I found something rare, purchase it, and put it on eBay only to realize there were 100,000 others just like it for sale.

I had to learn what to look for. I sold off collections of items from my grandmother and my mom that really helped me learn what to buy. Of course, at one point, I did get a bit desperate and decided to sell all of my husband's pants. That idea worked well for extra money, but when church rolled around the next week and he was looking for his khakis...well, let's just say it didn't sit well. It took all the extra money I had just made to go to the store and buy him another pair of pants!

EBay can also be tricky due to shipping costs and such, so be sure to do your research before you start. There are plenty of books at the library or online tutorials that can help you with this.

A couple years ago, I got into Craigslist as well. I used this mainly for purchasing. It is similar to an online garage sale—you find the item and then you have to go pick up the item. I grew tired of going to people's homes to pick up items I liked only to find that the item looked much better in the picture!

Use common sense here, too. Look out for scams. If you sell or buy an item, don't go alone. Take someone with you and meet at a public place. I've met a few shady people through Craigslist, but most of my experiences have been good.

Having a Garage Sale

Yes, it's old school advice. Do you know the very first garage sale I had with my husband, we made $900? Yep—that's mega money in the garage-sale world!

There are many ways to do this, the first being the most obvious: Clean out your house. Get those items out of the attic that you have been holding on to for no apparent reason—and sell them! Simplify. Gather up the toys, the clothes that don't fit, the books you never read, and all the VHS tapes, and then hold an old-fashioned garage sale.

The second way to do this is a little different: Actually buy things to sell. If you have an eye for good deals, then this is the way to go. You can visit other garage sales, flea markets, and so forth and find good deals where the seller is asking much less than she should. Buy the item and then resell it at your garage sale.

My dad used to buy storage units that had defaulted and sell them at a flea market and at our garage sales. When people stopped paying their payments on their unit, the unit went to auction and he'd buy them. Sometimes it was good and sometimes it wasn't.

I actually have family members who have made a *living* doing this. Recently, they turned in all the gold jewelry they had collected over the years from various auctions, sales, and so forth, and it was enough to buy a new car! Wow.

The treasure is out there; but like a pirate, you'll have to hunt for it!

Did you know you could also have a garage sale with your coupon finds? Now, I wouldn't recommend selling your boxes of Frosted Flakes, but I have been to many garage sales from fellow couponers. I've walked in to find tons of shampoo, deodorant, and all kinds of other things—all still in the packages and being sold at dirt-cheap prices.

Just think about it: You got it free, the store sells it for $3.00, and you sell it for $1.50. You are still cheaper than the stores, and you're making a profit from all that hard couponing! I always know when I'm walking into a couponer's garage sale because it feels like I'm walking into my own house!

If you do decide to have a garage sale, be sure to clean up your items. Sometimes you can even ask more for them because they are clean. A little soap can go a long way! Also, be sure to price them accordingly. I have walked into sales where used kids' clothes are priced $5.00 apiece, but as a deal hunter, I know I can probably buy my kids' clothes brand-new at the store for less than $5.00 apiece!

Reviewing Products

This is not a great way to make extra money, but it is a way to get products for free that you normally might not be able to purchase for yourself or for your family. The first website I started doing this for was BzzAgent.com, an amazing word-of-mouth marketing site that allows users to join a campaign, review a product, and spread the word. As I mentioned before, you then earn points for the review.

For me, the chance to get free products (not to mention coupons too) was a great opportunity. I've received makeup, cleaning products, a free subscription to a magazine, and much more. Plus, it is a very interactive website that becomes not only fun but addictive too!

As a stay-at-home mom, I had to get creative about saving money. The great thing is that as I prayed for wisdom in this area, God began to open door after door. Do you know at one point we even dragged out an old fan from our apartment complex dumpster, cleaned it up, and sold it for $50.00? It turned out to be a collector's item and we didn't even know it.

The previous list is of a few things that I have actually done for extra money, but of course you can always get a job or try making things at home and selling them. I've done those things, too, but what I needed at the time I started couponing was literally extra money I could make without ever leaving my house. And, praise God, the doors opened and opportunities came!

So there you have some extra ideas not just for saving money, but for making a little extra on the side—all things you can do while clipping away at coupons, having swap parties, and hunting for bargains at your local grocery or drug stores.

You probably have questions—I know I did when I got started. So although there's a ton of great information on my site, www.918couponqueen.com, let's look at some of the most popular here in the next chapter. I'd be willing to bet that some of these will help you out a lot.

Top 10 FAQs

"And God said, 'Let there be light,' and there was light"
(Genesis 1:3).

Chapter Highlights:

- Do You Take Good Deals, Even When You Don't Need the Item Right Away?
- How Does "Standing on the Word" Help Me Use a Few Coupons?
- This Seems Overwhelming. Is It Really Worth It?
- It Does Sound Really Complicated; Is It Going to Take Up All of My Time?
- What Do I Do If I Hit the Store and Forget My Coupons but I Can't Go Home?
- What Do I Do If I Only Have One Store in My Area at Which to Shop?

✂ Will I Hold Up the Line?

✂ I Did My First Shopping Trip but Still Spent a Lot of Money Building Up My Stockpile—Is This Normal?

✂ What About Warehouse Stores? Are Those Better for Deals?

✂ I Still Have Questions; Where Do I Go for Answers?

If you have been struggling to make ends meet, or if you have been searching for that one little thing that could bring in extra money for you and your family, you have found it in couponing! Couponing will help bring light to whatever dark financial situation you are going through, from the smallest to the biggest.

> *Couponing will help bring light to whatever dark financial situation you are going through, from the smallest to the biggest.*

After you become a pro at couponing, you can then apply that same mentality of "making a good deal better" to everything you do. Apply it to buying items at work or buying clothes for the kids—you can save money *anywhere* with these tips! I didn't stop simply at groceries; I applied the 918 Coupon Queen mind-set to everything that I purchased!

Now that you've read the basics on couponing, you're ready to join me and thousands of others in saving money. However, it's hard to give everyone everything they need in one book, and so I have taken this chapter to list some of the questions I get asked the most frequently.

The following questions are some of the most common questions I receive about couponing:

1. What if you see a good deal but you really don't need it; do you buy it anyway?

If I can afford to buy it, yes, I do! I can hold onto it for later...or maybe there's an even better option. Read what Tonya e-mailed me:

> I just wanted to say thank you!! With your guidance and wonderful tips, you have enabled me to help a family friend—something I could not do three months ago! He lost his job six months ago, and by accident we found out two days ago that he was having a hard time! My mom was going to see him again today, and my family was trying to help him any way they could. Money is tight for my entire family at this time, so for me, giving money was not feasible. However, I could give him something to eat. My mom left my house with three Walmart bags of groceries.
>
> Thank you! Without you, I could not have helped in this way! My mom called when she left him and told me he could not believe that we would help him in this way!

If you were to step outside your house right now and look to the left and then to the right, chances are, one of your neighbors is struggling financially. You may have picked up this book because you're struggling too, but the thing we have to remember is that we are not alone. But sometimes it can seem as though we are.

When my husband and I went through the financial strain of medical bills and just not having

Couponing is amazing not only for saving money but for opening doors to the ability to give back.

enough money to make it, we never told anyone. In fact, there are probably family members reading this book who did not realize some of the things we went through!

Chances are there are people around you who are just like us, suffering in secret. It is so hard for us, as humans, to take the focus off of ourselves and what we are going through and instead think about someone else. We tend to have the "poor me" attitude, or we can simply be so wrapped up in whatever our circumstances are that we do not see those around us that are hurting too.

Couponing is amazing not only for saving money but for opening doors to the ability to *give back*.

We are commanded to tithe, and then we are called to give. Giving is above and beyond the tithe. We are tithing in obedience to God's Word, and then as we walk in the Word we become led to give to others. We begin to sow seed into the lives of others.

This is why couponing is so amazing. Not only can you cut your grocery bill in half or more, but you can also give to others!

Are you waiting for a breakthrough? Are you waiting for a miracle that will set you free from whatever you are dealing with right now? Then give.

Obey God and honor Him with the tithe, and then sow seed into those around you. God will honor the seed you sow, and you will reap a harvest of more than enough. This is why couponing is so amazing. Not only can you cut your grocery bill in half or more, but you can also give to others!

Food is a basic necessity to life; you just won't survive long without it. Oftentimes, we think that giving means giving *money*.

But, really, buying someone groceries for a week is as if you handed them a hundred dollars or more!

After I had my first son, Elisha, people showered us with gifts! However, one of the best gifts I got was a week's worth of groceries from a friend of mine. She literally showed up with grocery sacks full of food. After I had a baby, it was all I could do to get across the *house,* let alone get to the store! It was one of the most thoughtful gifts I had ever received; it helped us so much by taking away the stress of having to get to the store and also helped us financially.

When you begin couponing, you will quickly find that you will be able to purchase items that are either free or almost free. As I've mentioned, I get almost all of my personal care items such as toothpaste, deodorant, shampoo, soap, and even makeup nearly free, and these are great items to donate to a charity or a family in need.

While stockpiling is something that I do advocate in order to save the most money, instead of stockpiling years' worth of food that mice can eat or that could go bad, I say we share it with those around us. Share with your neighbors or with your friends. Don't become a hoarder!

Honestly, I do not believe that we should have rooms and rooms full of "good deals." We should stock up for our own needs; however, if you have enough spaghetti to feed a small army, then it's time to pull out the grocery sacks and start spreading the wealth.

Pack up a bag full of groceries and take it next door to your neighbors and let it bless others around you. Remember, God said, *"Give, and it will be given to you..."* (Luke 6:38). That is a spiritual law, and if we want to receive God's blessing for us, then we will have to give.

Equally important, however, are the motives behind our giving. God sees the heart; He sees past all our fake smiles and Christian greetings and into the heart of the matter. Be careful not to give just to receive; give genuinely to help those around you!

I believe we have been missing the concept of helping one another, and more than that, I believe the world has taken notice of it. We are living in a very selfish time, and we're all thinking about just ourselves all the time. "What about my feelings?" "What about my money?" "What about what I want?" "What about my stuff?"

If you get your eyes off yourself and onto someone else, God will keep His eyes on you. God has your back!

If, as believers, we stood together and decided to stop looking at ourselves and to start each day thinking, *How can I help someone else today?* what would happen?

For a long time I thought, *If I think about someone else, then who is going to think about me?* Do you often feel that if you didn't take care of yourself, then no one would? That's just not true because if you get your eyes off yourself and onto someone else, God will keep His eyes on you. God has your back!

Our core purpose is to show others the love of Christ. How do you do that? Help others around you. You may not have a check to give or an extra hundred-dollar bill in your pocket, but when you start getting the hang of this couponing business, I assure you that you'll have groceries and other products that you have been able to purchase for next to nothing that can bless a family.

Even if you don't know someone personally, find a church or charity that you would like to be a part of and give. As you give to others, do you know what will happen to you? God says, *"Give, and it will be given to you. A good measure, pressed down, shaken together and running over, will be poured into your lap. For with the measure you use, it will be measured to you"* (Luke 6:38).

Yes, couponing may change your life and enable you to feed your family and meet your need to eat, but what's even better is when you have *more than enough!* Then you can take care of yourself and others too!

Ask God to put people in your path that you can give to. Start sowing seeds into other people and get your eyes off yourself and your circumstances. God has your back; He will not let you fall.

Remember what the Israelites said in the desert after God freed them from abuse, slavery, and death and then supernaturally delivered them from the Egyptians as they walked through the Red Sea: *"If only we had died by the LORD's hand in Egypt! There we sat around pots of meat and ate all the food we wanted, but you have brought us out into this desert to starve this entire assembly to death"* (Exodus 16:3).

After all God had done for them, they said, *You have brought us out into this desert to starve.* Really? God freed them from slavery, death, and evil, then supernaturally delivered them from their enemies by parting the Red Sea and allowed them to walk right through it. And they thought He'd let them starve.

Isn't it funny how we can suddenly forget the big picture and get our eyes on our circumstances?

God is in the business of giving, and, frankly, if that is God's business, then I want it to be my business as well.

We forget about all the unbelievable things God has done in our lives, and we only see our paycheck, the boss we don't like, the leak in the sink, etc.

It is time we began to see those around us and rise up as believers and be a witness for the Son of God who died for us. How can anyone see a difference in us if we're complaining and griping like everyone else? If we are stocking up our sixty-five boxes of Hamburger Helper while our neighbors sit in their houses praying that they can make it for another week, we are not showing them Jesus.

It just is not right. My methods of couponing make it so easy to give back to those around us, and I encourage you to do so— don't worry; God will give you more deodorant where that came from! God is in the business of giving, and, frankly, if that is God's business, then I want it to be my business as well.

2. How does standing on the Word help me use a few coupons?

I claim God's promises before I ever enter the store! We are believers, we should have the best, and you better believe I am out in that parking lot claiming good deals and favor when I am in that store!

I believe in standing on the Word and believing God's promises because couponing may change your life for the moment, but God will change your life forever!

If our God can split the sea and raise the dead, if He cares for sparrows and clothes lilies in beauty, then surely He will take care of me by sending a few good sales my way! As I honor the Lord, I walk in His supernatural favor everywhere I go, whether that is at my job or standing at the grocery store.

I believe in standing on the Word and believing God's promises because couponing may change your life for the moment, but God will change your life forever! If you want a life full of blessing and increase, then honor God and stand on His promises for your life while you're clipping the coupons!

3. This seems too overwhelming; is it really worth it?

Well, hopefully, by this point in the book you have realized that it is worth it, but just in case, here are a few examples for you:

Here's a Target deal from Mellissa:

> 10 Johnson's Buddies Soap
>
> 2 boxes of Kellogg's Pop-Tarts
>
> 1 box of Kellogg's Special K Bars
>
> 7 General Mills Individual Cereals
>
> 3 Dove Deodorants
>
> 1 kids' Colgate toothpaste
>
> 1 kids' Colgate toothbrush
>
> 6 boxes of Nexcare bandages
>
> Total after all coupons: **$7.75**.

Here's a quote from another one of our users, Becky:

"I went five times over the weekend with my kids and in all only spent $34.29 for $210.85 worth of stuff. You help me every day. I don't know what I would do without this website!!!!!"

Another one of our readers posted this deal:

"I got a jumbo pack of diapers, a pack of wipes, a bottle of Johnson & Johnson lotion and body wash, Aveeno baby lotion, an eight-pack of Good Start ready-to-feed bottles, one box of Kellogg's Pop-Tarts, two Gerber Yogurt Melts, and a three-piece plastic dining set for my son—all for the grand total of *$15.80!!!*"

Still think it's not worth it?

One of the greatest things about couponing is that it is mostly for name-brand, top-of-the-line products that you normally might not have been able to purchase!

These are just a few stories from moms around the country who have learned how to save money with coupons! One of the greatest things about couponing is that it is mostly for name-brand, top-of-the-line products that you normally might not have been able to purchase! I always tell people that once they do it and see the savings, they'll be hooked.

You can literally take the money you are saving and go on a vacation, get out of debt, or save it! I am a spender by nature, actually, and one of the things I enjoyed the most was that I was finally able to do things that I wanted to do but was not able to do on such a tight budget. I found myself being able to get my hair done again and get some new clothes— luxuries I did without for a long time! All the while, couponing for groceries and learning how to coupon for other things like clothing and shoes saved us enough money we could all eat with plenty left over!

4. **It does sound really complicated; is it going to take up all of my time?**

No. At first, it is going to take some time to get those coupons together and organized as you begin to find deals. But, over time, you will love it, and the amount of time you spend on it will become less and less.

There have even been a few times when I didn't plan my trip at all; I simply grabbed my coupons and headed out the door. I try not to do that often because it doesn't lead to the best deals, but I was still able to save a lot of money.

I have two very small children, and I can tell you if couponing were something that took all of my time, I would not do it either! It is a lot of fun, and in a short amount of time it can bring hundreds of dollars back into your home each month.

5. What do I do if I hit the store and forget my coupons but I can't go home?

That happens to the best of us. First, don't panic. If you can't go home and get your coupons, that's okay. Just grab the store flyer when you enter the store. Shop off the first page, especially, since that is where most of the Loss Leaders are located. Then walk around the store. Look for hidden sales and clearance racks. If you are there for ice cream, look at all the ice cream for a good sale or deal. Just because you forgot your coupons doesn't mean you still have to buy the most expensive brand of products.

Recently, I had to make an emergency trip to the grocery store for diapers, milk, and a few other staples. I did not realize we needed these things, so I did not bring my coupons with me, and since we live a bit outside town, going home to get them was not feasible.

I walked into the grocery store and grabbed the flyer right away. I quickly figured out which brand of milk was the least expensive. I walked over to the diaper area and grabbed a package of off-brand diapers. I do not normally buy those, but since that particular store had such high prices, I thought I would give them a try. I then walked around the store and found a few manager's specials and grabbed those for dinner.

All in all, I still saved money—even without my coupons. And, remember, you won't have coupons for everything you buy; there are times when you'll just have to settle for a sale. There's always a way to save; you just have to find it!

6. What do I do if I only have one store in my area at which to shop?

If you don't live close to a major metro area, it is quite possible that you have one option and one option only. I used to tell my preschoolers, "You get what you get and you don't throw a fit." If you only have one store, then you will have to maximize your savings at that one store.

> *"You get what you get and you don't throw a fit."*

Do a little detective work and find out every savings method available at that store. If you do live in a small town, talk with the owner or manager and see what they think about changing their coupon policy or even price-matching bigger chain store ads.

I once taught a class in a very small town, and the owner of the one grocery store was sitting in the class! I was able to share with her all of my money-saving tips and couponing tips, which she then took back to her store to use!

Sometimes living in a small town can mean better chances to save money if you just ask!

Also, if a bigger city is within reasonable driving distance, it may be worth it once a month to make a run to "the city" and snatch up deals at several stores at one time so you'll have enough to last you an entire month.

For example, if you drove to a bigger city maybe an hour away but you saved nearly $300 or more, then it might be worth it. Then all you need to purchase at your local high price store are perishables like milk or little things that you forgot to buy at the other stores.

Careful planning can really help out in this situation, and like I said, a small town may actually work to your advantage!

7. Will I hold up the line?

I once had a whole cart worth of groceries at a local Walmart. I also had my two kids and a handful of coupons to use. I noticed there was a woman behind me holding one Dr. Pepper. I quickly told her to go ahead of me. She looked at my cart and then back at me again and said, "No way. I don't know what you are about to do with those coupons but I want to watch you do it!" She stood there and watched my entire transaction just to see how much I would save!

I have to tell you that, normally, that is the kind of response I get. People literally stand back and watch. But, if I feel that the "deal" I am about to do is going to take some time, then I do politely ask if those behind me wish to go ahead of me.

Most of the time it all happens pretty fast, and it really doesn't hold the line up too long—computerized registers are a wonder! It's not that big of a deal to me anymore, and, frankly, if it is an issue for the person behind me, well, she can always find another line. I'm saving my money, and that is all there is to it!

If your store has a self-checkout, you can use your coupons there. But that can sometimes take even longer!

8. I did my first shopping trip but still spent a lot of money building up my stockpile—is this normal?

If you are starting from scratch and you are trying to build an entire stockpile overnight, then, yes, it is normal. However, you do not have to rush out tomorrow and purchase a house full of food! Start small! If you think this week is a great deal for cereal, then stock up on cereal. Just stockpile the deals you get after coupons and sales, not necessarily everything you see.

9. What about warehouse stores? Are those better for deals?

Not typically.

Insider's Tip: Most warehouse stores do not allow coupons.

You are simply paying for convenience. Many times the deal is about the same; it just looks better to you because of packaging and because it is at a warehouse, which always gives the appearance of being a good deal.

Warehouse stores are good for some things, though, such as prescriptions, fruit, dairy, and so forth. In fact, I bought my kitchen table from a warehouse store display. Bring your calculator and *know your prices.* Don't assume 500 Ziploc bags for only $8.00 is a good deal. If you had bought those in individual boxes at another store with your coupons, it might have only been $5.00.

10. I still have questions; where do I go for answers?

Questions are what 918 Coupon Queen Forums are *for!* I get tons of e-mails daily, and I cannot answer all of them—even though I do read them all. So, I suggest you become a member of www.918couponqueen.com (for free) and post your questions in our forums.

There are thousands of folks on our website that would love to hear your savings story and answer questions. Perhaps even you can help answer a few questions, too! I am also active on the forums, and I answer questions and post my deals as well.

Questions are what 918 Coupon Queen Forums are for!

Also, the daily blog at www.918couponqueen.com will provide tons of great deals, coupons, and sales for you each day. I update the information myself and post new deals just for you! Be sure to check out www.918couponqueen.com for more information!

CHAPTER 12

The Proverbs 31 Woman: It's More Than You Think

"She sees that her trading is profitable, and her lamp does not go out at night" (Proverbs 31:18).

As a stay-at-home mom in a financial crisis, I feel like I tried nearly everything to make extra money. However, the very first thing I did was pray for God to show me ways of bringing in extra money—but also I prayed for a *continual* method of increase.

This is important, because so many people want the mystery check that shows up in your mailbox and makes everything okay. Chances are, that's not going to happen. There were several times that I would go to the grocery store and beg God to send someone who would pay for my groceries as I checked out. It didn't work out like I'd hoped.

It's not that God can't do that; it's not that God *won't* do it, but sometimes there are things in life we have to go through so we can learn from them and move on to the next level that God has for us.

You'll learn to fish

Although it was hard at the time, looking back on it, if God would have sent someone to pay for my groceries, I never would have learned this remarkable technique, which I've been able to share with thousands of other folks going through exactly what I went through.

God was looking at the *big picture.* Even though I was dealing with the moment, I was also praying about the big picture. I did not want a miracle (not that it would have been a bad thing), I wanted a *continual method* of increase that would help my family for the rest of our lives. I didn't need someone bringing me the fish; I needed someone to teach me how to fish.

I literally prayed for opportunities of continual increase. I think that is where we miss it sometimes; we want the easy way out. And, because of that, the focuses of our prayers are for escape routes and nothing more. Picture your life as a highway: If all you do is spend your time looking for the nearest exit, you will never make it to your destination, which is all that God has in store for you.

I think that is where we miss it sometimes; we want the easy way out. And, because of that, the focus of our prayers is for escape routes and nothing more.

It goes against everything we feel inside, but staying the course and walking through life with God instead of depending on God to get you out of life allows Him to complete His work in you.

We all want prosperity; we all want health; we all want the best and want to leave the best for our children's children. The question is, do we want to do what it takes to get there?

You'll survive the desert

I have had the disconnect notices, I've answered the phone calls of debt collectors, and I've sat and wondered how on earth we were going to make it.

But, you know what? We're still here.

God never left us; He took us by the hand, and, even though it was hard, He led us through the wilderness. I do not want to get stuck in the desert. If you are a believer, know that God has His best in store for you. Know there is more to life than what you are seeing in your circumstances. So are you going to let Satan keep you in the desert?

I did have to get a bit creative, and I did have to think outside the box a bit, but you know what, God literally showed me things that I could do that would lead to increase. I was not able to get a job and my husband could not possibly take on another one— at the time, he was working two jobs and going back to school— but we made it!

You'll be like the Proverbs 31 woman

I read Proverbs 31 every day out loud. I've heard pastors say that there is no way a woman can live up to this example, but, honestly, I do not believe that is true. I believe we are called to be the "virtuous woman." It's not that we have to be perfect, but in essence, she was Christ-like and full of wisdom—why would that not be something we would want?

Proverbs 31:11 says this: *"Her husband has full confidence in her and lacks nothing of value."*

This one struck me quite hard when I first read it. The thought of my husband having confidence in me was something I had never heard of, considering that most of the teaching we hear is about wives trusting in their husbands as being the head of the household. Don't get me wrong, that is also true, but God was saying that trust and confidence is a two-way street. In this verse, her husband was confident in her, and because of that, he lacked nothing of value. He had everything he needed.

God was saying that trust and confidence is a two-way street.

The Amplified Bible says it this way: *"The heart of her husband trusts in her confidently and relies on and believes in her securely, so that he has no lack of [honest] gain or need of [dishonest] spoil"* (Proverbs 31:11).

This reinforces the fact that we as wives are to support our husbands (not necessarily financially but as helpmates), but it also tells us something more. The virtuous woman was doing something to assist the family finances in some way that caused her husband to lack nothing of value. Does this mean that your husband should have everything in life that he wants? Not necessarily—tell him not to get too excited about that new Italian sports car. What it does mean is that he is satisfied with what he has, and he is confident in his wife and her abilities.

What are her abilities?

She is like the merchant ships,
*   bringing her food from afar.*

She gets up while it is still dark;
she provides food for her family
and portions for her servant girls.

She considers a field and buys it;
out of her earnings she plants a vineyard.

She sets about her work vigorously;
her arms are strong for her tasks.

She sees that her trading is profitable,
and her lamp does not go out at night.

(Proverbs 31:14-18)

You're like a merchant ship

Let's start at the beginning, *"She is like the merchant ships, bringing her food from afar"* (v.14). She goes out and buys the food for the family. In a humorous way, I always thought, *Well, I am driving clear across town to buy our groceries this week; I suppose that means I am bringing our food from afar. I mean, do you have any idea how far Walmart is from my house!?!*

I think, though, the basis of this means that she is taking care of her family, which is what we have been called to do.

You're not lazy and have enough

"She gets up while it is still dark; she provides food for her family and portions for her servant girls" (v. 15).

Two things to notice here:

1. The virtuous woman is not lazy; she rises early and takes care of her family and servants. This is not to say

Our God is a God of more than enough!

that you can't sleep in every once in a while, but I think it describes us as wives and mothers very well—we are constantly busy looking out for our families.

2. Servant girls—she had enough that she was also able to keep help and provide for *them* as well. Praise God that our God is a God of more than enough! Although most of us do not have servants these days, God had certainly blessed this family with enough money and food to provide for extra help. A friend of mine jokes that her washer and dryer and other appliances are her "servants"! It also tells us that she did not do everything alone.

You're going to get help

I feel like God has been laying that concept on my heart a lot these days—the virtuous woman had help. It is okay to ask for help; you're not super woman, and you cannot do everything yourself. I struggle constantly with agreeing to volunteer for something, having a party for something, or going somewhere for somebody—even when I know that I do not have time to do that right now. I overextend myself...and my husband and kids suffer for it.

> *I overextend myself...and my husband and kids suffer for it.*

I end up getting short with them, losing my temper, and being completely stressed out—all in the name of helping someone else. Sometimes, we just have to say "no."

And we have to ask for help.

I am so blessed to have become the 918 Coupon Queen, but it does require quite a bit of work. It takes lots of time and energy to build a website, update it daily, teach workshops, monitor e-mails, handle social media, and have weekly news segments. In the beginning, I did all of this with my kids at home with me. It was very difficult.

I knew God's hand was on this business, and I knew doors were opening that I needed to step through, but I could not handle the idea of letting someone else watch my children. God knew that too. Not too long after 918 Coupon Queen exploded, my parents began to build a home only a mile away from mine! Thankfully, I have a great family, and having them close by has been a real blessing. It took a while, but I eventually broke down and asked for help—and now for a few hours each week, my mother watches the boys while I work.

I think if the woman in Proverbs 31 can have help, so can we. Ask God to lead you in the right direction toward the help you need...and the humility to ask. Even if that just means a babysitting trade-off with a friend, we just can't do it all.

You're going to make wise business decisions

"She considers a field and buys it; out of her earnings she plants a vineyard" (v. 16).

This is a woman making business decisions that will bless her family. She is confident; she sees a good deal, weighs the pros and cons, and acts. These business ventures develop out of her earnings, and she plants a vineyard, that will prove to be another good business decision and provide for her family with lasting income.

This was important to me because I knew in my heart that God was going to give me a business idea. So, what did I do? I went out and tried to find one myself. I've sold vitamins, I've sold makeup, and I seriously considered selling pots and pans (even though I can hardly use one). It is not that those things are bad; however, instead of waiting on God to bring the ideas, I jumped out and tried to move God along a bit.

Lo and behold, those things not only did not make me money—they actually *cost* me a great deal of money. I knew without a shadow of a doubt that there was something out there I just had not found yet that I was supposed to do. I did not know what it was.

> *I jumped out and tried to move God along a bit. Lo and behold, those things not only did not make me money—they actually cost me a great deal of money.*

Looking back on it now, the reason why I couldn't just jump out and grab a business was that the business God had for me required me to walk through a bit of life before I could effectively start it.

I needed to learn how to live with a financial strain, I needed to learn how to be victorious, and more than that, I needed to learn who it was that would bring the victory!

As you are looking for ways to save money and/or earn money, pray to God and ask for wisdom. Ask God to show you what it is that you are supposed to do that will bring wealth into your family.

You're a blessing to your husband

At the same time, pray for your spouse. Pray that he will find what he is supposed to do in this life and be satisfied with it and that the work of his hands will be blessed. Also, ask God that He minister to your husband as He reveals what your own purpose is and that your spouse will be supportive of what God is showing you. Pray for unity, for you and your husband should be on the same page. God is not in the business of pulling families apart, so be sure to listen to your spouse's concerns.

My husband has been 100 percent supportive of all of my business adventures. However, if I had listened to some of the concerns he had, it would have saved us a lot of trouble and money.

My husband has been 100 percent supportive of all of my business adventures. However, if I had listened to some of the concerns he had, it would have saved us a lot of trouble and money.

God has a plan for you; in fact, God says, *"'For I know the plans I have for you,' declares the LORD, 'plans to prosper you and not to harm you, plans to give you hope and a future'"* (Jeremiah 29:11). Start praying that God reveal His purpose for your life, and start praying according to the Word!

Proverbs 31:16 says that the virtuous woman considers a field, which means she thought about it, prayed about it, and made sure it was the right thing to do. Don't jump into something headfirst without considering the risks and your family!

There are people in this life who are risk takers; they dive in with everything they have. That may be easy to do when you are single, but when you have a family, things change. It is important to use wisdom and be sure that it is God's will for you and your family.

You're strong

"She sets about her work vigorously; her arms are strong for her tasks" (Proverbs 31:17).

Again, this scripture reinforces that this woman is not lazy—she works hard. If you want to see your seed turn into a harvest, it's going to take a bit of work.

I am not a farmer, but what I do know is that they do not simply throw the seed out onto the ground and then come back a few months later to a beautiful harvest. Farmers have to sow the seed. Meaning, they have to clear the land, make sure the soil is good, dig, and plant the seeds. Then they have to maintain the field, keeping away the animals, bugs, and weeds that try to destroy their crops.

> *Listen: You have planted your seeds by tithing, praying, and being obedient to the Word of God. And while you are waiting for a harvest, you are going to endure a few animals, bugs, and weeds that seek to destroy what God is doing in your life.*

Listen: You have planted your seeds by tithing, praying, and being obedient to the Word of God. And while you are waiting for a harvest, you are going to endure a few animals, bugs, and weeds that seek to destroy what God is doing in your life.

This woman worked hard, just like the farmers do. Day in and day out they are in their fields maintaining and watering their crops and sowing seed for a blessed harvest. If you want to reap what you sow, then you better sow good seed and work hard to keep the enemy away!

Sitting in your house each day complaining because you don't have this or that, wishing that you had a big business, a nice car, and some new clothes while letting everyone around you know how miserable you are will not bring increase into your life. In fact, you might as well buy a comfortable chair, because you won't be moving anywhere for a long time to come!

You're going to reap what you sow

Sowing and reaping is a spiritual law. God set up His kingdom to work in this way. God won't change His Word for you. You have to make up your mind that you are going to have to work hard to see good results from the seeds you have sown.

My husband and I have always tithed. We were brought up that way, and when we got married, we continued to tithe—no questions asked. As we got older, though, we also realized that we could sow seed in addition to what we were tithing—either in offerings or sowing *time* into other people or by giving away things we had to others.

We know the Word, and we know that we are blessed. So many believers start out tithing...and then the storms come. Something in your house breaks, the car gets wrecked, or the kids need new clothes—something inevitably happens. And, instead of praying to God for wisdom about taking care of these things, many believers take from the tithe.

Do you know how God views this? Theft! Malachi 3:8 says this: *"Will a man rob God? Yet you rob me. But you ask, 'How do we rob you?' In tithes and offerings."*

Too many believers take from the tithe, then sit back and wonder why they are not being blessed. They blame the church, blame their

Water it daily with the Word of God, keep watch over it with prayer, and give thanks for it with worship; and then you'll reap your harvest!

family, blame even God, and never look at themselves. Tithing is a commandment given to us from God; again, God will not change His Word for us—it is and always will be the same.

What we have to learn is that when we sow the seed, the enemy is going to come and try to take it. You're going to have to maintain what you sow and work hard to keep it. Water it daily with the Word of God, keep watch over it with prayer, and give thanks for it with worship; and then you'll reap your harvest!

You're going to be rewarded for your hard work

"She sees that her trading is profitable, and her lamp does not go out at night" (v.18).

This woman has done several things by this point:

1. She is not lazy
2. She asked for help
3. She makes wise decisions
4. She invests in her family
5. She works hard

It is because she has done these things that her trading is profitable. Profit does not come easy; it takes a lot of hard work. As she is seeing profit, what does she do? She continues to work at it.

Many times people will work hard and gain success in hopes of riding the wave of success and never having to work at it again. Most of the time, success lasts for a moment, but if you want it to continue, you'll have to continue working at it.

Farmers must be thinking ahead... and so must we.

Look at the farmers again. They sow the seed, maintain the fields, and reap the harvest. But what happens next year? They start the cycle all over again. The harvest they reap is temporary, and, in fact, as soon as they harvest the crop, they are already working on next year's crop! Farmers must be thinking ahead...and so must we.

When you are reaping your harvest, pray that God shows you how to *maintain those fields* so that you will be *continually* reaping a harvest. Those who have been farming for a long time can tell you exactly what you need to do to keep certain animals, bugs, and weeds out of your field. And, over time, because they know how to resist those things, the threat seems to diminish.

The same is true in our lives. As we learn how to resist Satan, over time when Satan hits us, instead of complaining, crying, and not knowing what to do, we immediately come back with the Word and stand strong knowing that God is on our side.

You're going to successfully resist the enemy

We read, *"Submit yourselves, then, to God. Resist the devil, and he will flee from you"* in James 4:7. If you don't want to deal with critters eating up your seeds, then you had better learn how to fight the critters. How do you fight the enemy?

1. Submit to God

2. Resist the devil

Stand on the Word, pray the Word, speak the Word—it was given to you as the "sword of the Spirit" (Ephesians 6:17), as we talked about earlier. Would a warrior go to battle without his sword? No! Neither should we.

When you get to the point of "seeing your trading as profitable," be sure to gear up, because chances are as long as you are alive the devil will still be coming after you.

Does this mean we have to live afraid of the devil? No! Does this mean that the devil is always going to take my profit? No. There is nothing sharper than the sword God gave us for battle. In fact, the Bible says, *"For the word of God is living and active. Sharper than any double-edged sword, it penetrates even to dividing soul and spirit, joints and marrow; it judges the thoughts and attitudes of the heart"* (Hebrews 4:12).

Jesus stayed forty days in the desert being tempted by Satan himself, and how did He resist? He pulled out the sharpest sword ever made. And then what happened? *"The devil left him"* (Matthew 4:11).

As you learn to stand on God's Word and trust in Him, the attacks will get easier and easier to *resist;* it is almost as if the devil realizes he just can't get to you. It doesn't mean that he won't every now and again, but, overall, you'll see the victory because you are standing on the Rock.

You're going to be a doer, not a wisher

Sow good seed, maintain the fields, protect the seed, reap the harvest, and then sow more seed. Be on your guard and work hard and God will *"bless all the work of your hands"* (Deuteronomy 28:12).

These things are just as true for men as they are for women, but the only side I truly know is the woman's side of things. Being in the home, taking care of the children, and knowing that God has more in store for me than what we were seeing inspired me to take a closer look at Proverbs 31 than I had ever done before. Suddenly, I saw it as something attainable and a goal rather than something I only wished I had.

I think we spend too much time wishing and not enough time doing. God led me one step at a time. It began simply with helping to feed my own family; then I began to learn how to save money on everything, not just clothes. All of the sudden I developed a talent for being frugal—notice I did not say cheap, I said frugal.

> *I think we spend too much time wishing and not enough time doing.*

You're going to have good ideas

Inspired by a friend, I tried teaching my "smart shopping strategies" at a community center. As it turns out, people rather liked it, and so did I. One step at a time, God opened doors. I did not have to push them down; I did not have to take anyone over or step on anyone along the way. God opened the doors.

I began a free website; literally, I did not spend a dime to start it. I decided since one community center liked me, maybe others would too. So, I called them *all*. I began teaching classes at a local community college and all the community centers that would allow me in. I then spoke about my website, which was not much at that time.

I began to pray and ask God how I could expand my business. I ordered free business cards through an online deal and made some cute flyers to pass around. Then I got an idea to ask my mom and my sister to e-mail news stations and newspapers to help spread the word. Within a week, I had a newspaper article and a TV interview.

The women who owned www.918moms.com saw my newspaper article and asked me to come aboard. Soon after, I had a website, weekly news segments, radio spots, sold-out classes, and monthly articles.

God gave me an idea, and He led me step-by-step; it wasn't a leap, it wasn't a "risk all" move. It was one step at a time. When I was fully standing on one step, God opened a door to the next one. It has not all been easy, and it certainly has taken me out of my comfort zone and into a world I did not expect to be in.

When I was in high school, I used to throw up if I knew I was going to have to talk in front of the class; sometimes I would get the answer wrong if I had to answer a question out loud, simply because I was so nervous.

It amazes me today that I can speak in front of a crowd of people without throwing up or passing out. Isn't it funny what God can do if we just let Him?

You're going to get more from God than you will couponing

Maybe you have lost your job, or maybe you just need a little extra money. Couponing will help you tremendously—it will bring in extra money and definitely increase your finances. However, couponing cannot come close to doing in your life what God can do.

Couponing cannot come close to doing in your life what God can do.

God took the sickness Satan threw at us and the financial mess we were drowning in and made it a business that is teaching thousands of people how to feed their families and bring up their children knowing the responsibility of saving money and spending wisely. There is more to life than coupons and more to life than the economic situation that you are in. God is bigger than your circumstances.

It can be hard because at times the light at the end of the tunnel looks more like a lightning bug, but the more you trust God and obey His Word, the bigger that light becomes—until it is so bright, there is no darkness left to be seen!

I was born and raised in a Christian family; I've grown up in the church. Let me just say, at this point, I've seen too much of God to deny that He exists or to think that He is out to get me. I know who is out to get me, and God is not him. I know who brings sickness, who steals joy and finances, and I know it is not God.

You're going to have abundant life

Jesus tells us, *"The thief comes only to steal and kill and destroy; I have come that they may have life, and have it to the full"* (John 10:10).

As believers, it is time for us to rise up and start standing on the Word of the God we claim to believe in. It is time for us to stop giving up our families, our finances, and our health and take them back in the name of Jesus! I do not want to go through this life wishing I had something better. Jesus said He came that we may not only have life but have it more abundantly (John 10:10 NKJV)!

Same old same old isn't doing it for me anymore—I want the life Jesus died for me to have! Let's reach out and take hold of it!

Don't let your words counteract what God wants to do in your life. If something comes against you, watch your mouth! Do you really need to call everyone in town and tell them how sick you feel? Get rid of that "poor me" attitude!

I know a woman who calls every single time something in her life goes wrong. It is as if she wants me to feel as bad as she does. Even if some of her complaints are legitimate problems, it is awfully hard to feel bad for her when she is constantly telling me only of her problems. Everything in me just wants to scream, "Get over it!" The sad part is that until she does learn how to get over it and move on, she will continue to experience a life of problems.

Satan knows how to get her, and why would he fix something if it's not broken? He knows how to keep her down, and he'll keep doing it until she gets a revelation and gets over it.

I think it is time we all get over a few things. A friend of mine once said to her husband, "Put your big boy pants on and get over it!" I nearly fell over laughing, and how true it is!

Yes, there are things in life that are horrible, and I realize how difficult it can be to walk through certain circumstances. I am not trying to make light of those situations; however, I believe we serve a God who is bigger than our circumstances.

You're going to stand on the Word

I feel like sometimes when I teach workshops and talk about "standing on the Word," people just look at me and think, *Isn't that just charismatic jargon?*

I think it's unfortunate that we can throw phrases and words around so much in the Christian world that they lose their meaning. But as Christians we're supposed to place our faith in God's promises and stand on the Word, no matter what our denomination is!

How do you stand on the Word? It is simple. Search the Bible and find scriptures that resonate in your own life. Start saying those scriptures out loud in the face of defeat.

When something goes wrong in your house, don't gripe! Let Philippians 4:19 come out of your mouth: *"And my God will meet all your needs according to his glorious riches in Christ Jesus."* If you have to yell it to make yourself believe it, then yell it!

Anytime something comes your way, start falling to your knees instead of falling over.

In the *New King James Translation,* John 10:10 says, *"The thief does not come except to steal, and to kill, and to destroy. I have come that they may have life, and that they may have it more abundantly."* We are believers in Christ Jesus, and He died for us on the cross so that we can have life and have it more abundantly! The Bible actually says "abundantly"!

Are you living an abundant life? "Abundant" means present in great quantity; more than adequate; oversufficient; well supplied; abounding; richly supplied. Does that sound like your life?

If not, then you are not living the life Jesus died for you to have. It is time we lay down our old lives and take hold of the lives Jesus died for! I do not want to live another minute in torment, despair, and depression. I want the life that Jesus wants for me! And I want that for you and your family, too!

That includes having enough food, and—brace yourselves— enough money to pay the bills *and then some!* Not just pay the bills and be out of money, but pay them and then have some left over!

I am a believer in the Word; I tithe; I stand on the Word; I am a giver; and I have life and have life more abundantly! You do too!

Get up off your couch, go into your kitchen, open up those empty cabinets and open that empty refrigerator, and say out loud right now:

"I have plenty to eat until I am full, and I praise the name of the Lord my God, who has worked wonders for me" (Joel 2:26)! Amen!

---

i   1 Peter 2:9

ii   cf. Colossians 2:15

iii   cf. Romans 16:20, Ephesians 1:22

iv   Matthew 6:33

v   James 4:7

9 781932 503869